MW01253951

HOOKED ON A DRUMBEAT

A REAL LIFE EXPERIENCE

BY RON JOHNSON

Order this book online at www.trafford.com/08-0662
or email orders@trafford.com

Most Trafford titles are also available at major online book retailers.

© Copyright 2008 Ron Johnson
2006 Writer's Drumbeat
Edited by Daryl Currie
Photography by Ron Johnson
Cover sketch by Jerry Prusak
All rights reserved. No part of this publication may be reproduced, stored in a retrieval system, or
transmitted, in any form or by any means, electronic, mechanical, photocopying, recording, or
otherwise, without the written prior permission of the author.

Note for Librarians: A cataloguing record for this book is available from Library
and Archives Canada at www.collectionscanada.ca/amicus/index-e.html

Printed in Victoria, BC, Canada.

ISBN: 978-1-4251-7917-5

*We at Trafford believe that it is the responsibility of us all, as both individuals
and corporations, to make choices that are environmentally and socially sound.
You, in turn, are supporting this responsible conduct each time you purchase a
Trafford book, or make use of our publishing services. To find out how you are
helping, please visit www.trafford.com/responsiblepublishing.html*

*Our mission is to efficiently provide the world's finest, most comprehensive
book publishing service, enabling every author to experience success.
To find out how to publish your book, your way, and have it available
worldwide, visit us online at www.trafford.com/10510*

www.trafford.com

North America & international
toll-free: 1 888 232 4444 (USA & Canada)
phone: 250 383 6864 ♦ fax: 250 383 6804
email: info@trafford.com

The United Kingdom & Europe
phone: +44 (0)1865 487 395 ♦ local rate: 0845 230 9601
facsimile: +44 (0)1865 481 507 ♦ email: info.uk@trafford.com

10 9 8 7 6 5 4 3

This book is dedicated to
Mom and Dad
Who have been forever there

Acknowledgements

My sincere gratitude goes out to every character mentioned in this book. Whether I have presented your part in a positive light or otherwise, this story would not exist without your role in it. The story's focus is on events and human character, and for that reason, most last names have not been included. As well, some names have been changed for various reasons.

Thank you one and all for the experience.

To get this story into written form took prodding and assistance from all corners.

My immediate family has been a constant source of encouragement.

Shirley Neufeld, my lady, my love, has not only supported me during this undertaking, but has endured numerous readings of the manuscript correcting my errors.

My editor, Daryl Currie, provided the guidance I needed to make the story flow without embellishing the facts.

Mike O'Sullivan, my lifelong friend, and his wife Betty, have been constantly cheering me on, and this has played a major role in my completing the task.

And finally, thank you to all the friends of Bill W. This journey would not have transpired if it weren't for you.

Prologue

One day, in the late fall of 1991, I found myself sitting at the kitchen table staring at a crumpled piece of paper. The words scribbled on it years earlier represented those burning desires I hoped to fulfil before life's end. The itemized list had only a couple of check marks on it, such as the one alongside 'parachuting.' The unchecked items were a glaring reminder that my dreams were floating by. Forty-two years old, and the rut of life was pulling me in deeper and deeper. I was overcome with an enigmatic urge to break free from that suction.

Life is full of choices, and when one is chosen, another is left behind. Therefore, this is how I came to trade in serenity, security and a systematic way of life for one of adventure and uncertainty. The key to victory now lie in doing this without regrets.

The path that this decision led me on surpassed any expectation I may have had. Reliving the experience here, I have found no reason to embellish the facts. The tale that unfolded is at times even difficult for me to believe. Yes, truth can be stranger than fiction.

I am real, not ideal
The day my drumbeat matches His,
Then, maybe, then.......

Ron Johnson

PART I

Chapter 1

"Brazil, are you sure?" my father asked as he attempted to hide the concern in his voice.

"I don't know, just wanna live somewhere in South America. Life is passing me by and I have a lot of adventure left in this restless heart of mine," I replied.

"What about your good job? And wife? What happened?"

"Quit my job. We're getting a divorce. I'm gonna to do what I want and she's gonna to do what she wants. We're still friends, just our goals are different now," I said.

"Well, at least take a look at going to Venezuela. I think it's a little more stable there," my father said.

The intense fog was disconcerting. The last month and a half had been spent leading up to this moment, and now the grey mass in the air could very well impede my plans. My ex-wife stood at my side, ready to bid me farewell. We had both shed many a tear over my rash decision and now all that remained was the final good-bye. So there we stood, staring into the fog, making small talk and trying to put on a brave face as both of us prepared to face life apart. A good seven years of marriage had just dissolved when my adventurous spirit overrode logic, causing me to discard a good career, marriage and any notion of stability. The Amazon beckoned. Wanderlust, the subtle foe, had prevailed.

The sound of a plane interrupted a myriad of thoughts coursing through my mind. From the window of the terminal, all that was visible was fog – deep, intense fog. Then a shadow appeared like a ghost, low to the ground, passing quickly from east to west. The sound of jet engines resonated in the otherwise quiet setting. The reverberation was not one of landing, but of acceleration. With that came a heavy feeling in my chest, one of extreme disappointment, anxiety and apprehension. A voice announced over the PA system that the plane was unable to land in the thick fog so had proceeded north to its next stop. The plane would attempt to land again on the return. I began to sense that maybe this was some kind of omen. Was God trying to tell me something?

Back trying to make small talk, the unease within me magnified considerably. It was time: say the final good- bye, trust God to have the plane land on the rebound, and set my ex free to return to her new life, one without me. We embraced for the last time, I placed a kiss on her cheek, and she was gone.

Now alone, the feeling of freedom I wanted so desperately still eluded me, as I was neither on the plane nor out of town yet. The next hour I spent pacing, totally at the mercy of nature. The fog continued to mock my impatience, testing my resolve and threatening the outcome of events.

The plane was expected to return within half an hour, yet the fog showed no sign of lifting. Then, with only about ten minutes remaining, the mist magically began to dissipate. I was overwhelmed with a wondrous sense of awe at this miracle, which was further compounded by the sound of the 737 returning, right on time. Through the remnants of fog, the jet descended, alleviating a host of fears and setting free the turmoil I harboured inside.

I boarded the plane, and in minutes, we were airborne. I nestled into my seat, relaxed, and prepared to make the final break from traditional values. No longer did I have a home to maintain, a travel trailer to winterize, a motorbike to service or a vehicle to care for. A very profound insight overcame me as I realized that I had not owned all those things – they had owned me. My possessions had required attention, and in some cases, they had become an ongoing financial burden. The banker and I had dissolved our partnership and I was now free, truly free. With only one large pack of belongings left to my care, I let the jet propel me away from the material world below.

I have always enjoyed change but this time I knew I was pushing the limits. Not only was I about to face a new job, but a strange country and language as well.

The irony in the name of my new employer, Destiny Drilling, wasn't lost on me. I now found myself wondering what *my* destiny had in store for me. The owner, Adrian, was looking for someone with computer and administrations skills who would be willing to accept the various challenges of working on oil seismic projects throughout Venezuela. Adrian and I made a handshake deal and I agreed to pay my own airfare.

Absent, surprisingly, was any element of fear. Nor did I feel any resentment or regret. I leaned back in the plane's seat and let my mind wander back over my past and I began to reminisce.

———•◦•———

Ten years previously I had experienced a life-altering change when I finally bottomed out on a lifetime of booze and drugs. In desperation, I had reached out for help, and to my surprise, there were people ready and willing to help guide me out of that world of despair. They belonged to a twelve-step program that provided a guide to living that sounded a lot better than the manual I had been using so far. Thus began a fantastic journey and adventure like none other. Through that program, I gained sobriety, found a new purpose in life and a will to live. Most of all, I found out that there was a God, although not the kind I had previously perceived. Coincidences suddenly became miracles. Life had meaning and value. Things happened for a reason. I learned that life was what you make it and my past choices had made my world pure hell. The alternative option was to pursue a life of happiness. The choice was now mine.

Years of bad decisions had taken their toll. The saddest casualty was my common-law marriage, which had digressed to such grim state that a break became inevitable. One day in April of 1981, I left Ontario and headed west to my hometown of Peace River, Alberta, with my two-year-old son at my side.

I revelled in my new role of being a single parent, never imagining what a precious gift that would be. This, coupled with my newfound sobriety, provided me with the most exciting years of my life. The concept of accepting responsibility for a young child, and to not run away from each adversity, was novel for this vagabond. The problems I mounted became stepping-stones to growth, placing me on the path to maturity.

An opportunity to work in a correctional facility presented itself. This had turned out to be a dream career, one full of challenge and opportunity. Life's bounty continued to unfold when a wonderful lady named Shirley entered our lives. She had a daughter named Jackie who was nearly the same age as my son Shaine. We had an awe-inspiring wedding and bonded our two families together. Everything just kept getting better and better.

As I paused in my reflections, and peered down at the billowy clouds below, I couldn't help but wonder about the magnificence of it all. Smaller than a speck of dew in the scheme of things, I had somehow gained the attention of the powerful Being that had created the clouds and the sky they were in. Over time I have called Him many things: the Source, Friend, Creator, Great Spirit and God. Once I decided to receive guidance from this Entity, positive changes began to occur.

The hum of the plane soon had me lulled back into my reflective mood. Exactly, how was it that I came to be sitting on a plane headed off to the unknown?

"Shaine has decided he wants to stay here." With those words from Shaine's mother, my world came tumbling down. My son had gone for his annual summer vacation with his mother, without a hint of discontent with his present living situation. At the tender age of eight, he suddenly became master of his own destiny.

Many feared such a catastrophe would lead me back to my old life of booze and drugs. Family and friends held their breath while supporting me through this crisis. This was especially so with the support of my wife Shirley, without whom I'm sure I never would have made it through that trying time.

Since Shaine was adamant and did not vary in his desire, I had to practice what the program had taught me, to 'Let Go, and Let God.' He went to live with his mother, whose home was an eleven-hour drive from mine. Logistics dictated that instead of sharing life and love with my son daily, I would have to console myself with seeing him just two times a year. Although his absence was devastating, I was consoled by the fact that I knew he was going to a safe place full of love.

The negative feelings that consumed me affected every area of my life. Everything seemed to stagnate, the job, the marriage and even my program of sobriety. One day, out of desperation, I went up into the hills, got on my knees and prayed. I asked God to remove all hate and resentment and let forgiveness enter my heart. It was a life-changing moment, as I felt the weight of resentment lifted from me. I returned to town relieved of the burden that had weighed so heavily on my soul over the last couple of years.

Now, feeling a new sense of freedom, I entered a new chapter in my life. Some would call it a mid-life crisis. I possessed a long list of unfulfilled desires, I was in my early forties and my wish list wasn't getting any smaller.

So I made some drastic decisions. I quit my job, got a divorce and sold all my material possessions. Now, sitting on an airplane headed south, I didn't know what lay ahead, but for the first time in a long while, I felt truly alive. It was a great feeling to be finally following my own drumbeat.

Chapter 2

THE PLANE TOUCHED down in Phoenix, and faithfully there to greet me were my folks. They had met my many planes, trains and buses throughout the years, each time sparking a warm, fuzzy feeling within me. The Arizona sun warmed my cold bones and reassured me my new journey had truly begun. After an exchange of warm hugs and words, my parents and I embarked on finding a Spanish tutor at the University of Arizona. It was there we found Hugo, an adult student, who was willing to accept our mandate, and thus the lessons began.

When I originally decided to go to South America, I had no job prospect. I planned to go to Brazil and take whatever opportunity came my way. However, upon informing my parents of this decision and after the shock of the unforeseen change waned, my father had suggested I consider Venezuela instead. He felt it was a more stable country.

"Ron, wake up, you're not going to believe this," was how Dad roused me one particular morning. "There has been a coup in Venezuela."

"Get serious. You told me Venezuela was a stable country. Quit joshing me."

"No, I'm serious. Come look at the TV."

Watching the events unfold at my destination seemed like an absurd dream. But why now? Was this an omen? What was the message here; turn back, or continue following the incessant drumbeat pounding deep within my soul? Was this just a test to check my resolve?

Prayer, meditation and contemplation led me to conclude that I would indeed proceed, and just hope that things settled down by the time I arrived in Caracas. I was rather surprised at my lack of fear. It was as if the only path for me was straight ahead. With greater resolve than ever before, I decided to continue on to the land of Simon Bolivar.

The Spanish lessons were an experience in themselves. The tutor was of Mexican descent. He wheeled an old, step-side Chevy pickup and drove as if the road was his alone. And this man was no youngster!

"How many times have you had a gun pulled on you," I asked him one day as we careened through the streets of Phoenix.

"Only once," he replied, a big grin spreading across his face. "But, they didn't shoot."

I found this hard to believe, as his driving antics were so atrocious. Despite the radical trips through the city, the Spanish lessons progressed quite successfully. Hugo taught me the conjugation of verbs, keeping in mind that the type of work ahead in Venezuela would require talking to educated people such as lawyers and engineers. We had meals with Hugo's family, holding conversations in Spanish. These sessions continued for the duration of my three weeks in Mesa and helped immensely to build my confidence for what lay ahead.

Time spent with Mom and Dad was very relaxed. Along with my Aunt Bobby and Uncle Henry, we took in the movie, 'The Medicine Man', which I perceived to be another subliminal message. There was some good-natured jesting following that show.

"No," I informed them, "I'm not going down to demolish the rain forest."

I even managed to get in some twelve-step meetings conducted in Spanish, another method of working on the new language. As I listened intently, I was comforted that the language of the heart spoke to me regardless of idioma. This training aid further added to my growing self-assurance.

When the time came for the great departure, I was well rested, revitalized and focused on the destination ahead. Tremendous feelings of excitement and anticipation poured through me, begging to be vented.

The trip to the airport was no doubt one of great apprehension for my parents. Though conscious of their sentiments, I was hooked on a drumbeat; it was time to march on.

"I can't thank you enough, Mom, Dad, for standing behind me on this trip. I know it must be hard for you to understand me sometimes but you know me..."

"We certainly do. Just be careful," they said in unison.

After good-byes were said, I boarded the airplane and was off to Miami. With some ado, I managed to find the right concourse and got onto the correct plane to Caracas.

I was pleasantly surprised that they permitted smoking on the airplane. Freedom was what I was searching for, and this was a good start. I welcomed any diminishing of North American restrictions with an open heart. Little did I know that a very different set of limitations awaited just over the horizon.

Wanting to do everything correctly, I had been preparing extensively for this leg of the journey. I had purchased an open-ended ticket, much more expensive than other types, but one that could get me out of the country at any time. My passport was in order. I had an International Drivers License, Visa Card, cash on hand, and money in the bank. An acquaintance from my hometown had made some recent trips to Venezuela and had advised me how to obtain a taxi, how much to pay for it, a good hotel to stay at and how to work with the currency. My program had taught me to live one day at a time yet plans have to be made. The secret is not to plan the results. Yes, I was ready.

The best laid plans of mice and men were soon to unravel. The travel agent informed me that I would receive a tourist visa form on the plane, which I would need to fill out. Dick, my hometown acquaintance, advised me to fill out the proposed stay as a 90 tourist.

So, where were these visas? The plane was only an hour from landing yet no visa and my confidence, not unlike the fog, was starting to dissolve.

"We don't have enough tourist visas to go around, so you will have to get one when we arrive in Caracas. Sorry for the inconvenience," announced the stewardess

My anxiety set in again. This wasn't in the plan. I needed time to fill out the Spanish form because I feared I wouldn't be able to interpret it. The plane started its descent and the trepidation grew. It had been a long day, twenty hours in length, and far from over.

As anticipated, there was utter confusion upon disembarking, but there was one unexpected relief. A Venezuelan accosted me between the airplane and customs and offered his assistance in filling out my visa. Fatigue was setting in, so I gratefully accepted his help and slipped him a twenty-dollar bill. At this stage of the game, I did not feel like haggling price. I had but one goal and that was to get through the pandemonium. Upon arriving at the customs wicket, I discovered that no one spoke English. The customs agent, however, was courteous and fast. I quickly found myself in Venezuela with a ninety-day tourist visa in hand. Well, almost in country. First I had to retrieve my luggage.

Porters hovered around me like a swarm of bees, soliciting me in staccato Spanish for the obvious task of carrying my gear. I busily fended them off while impatiently waiting for my bag; it contained the sum of my worldly belongings. Finally, it fluttered onto the carousal and I forced my way through the multitude to retrieve it. Once I had it on the cart, I had to stand in line to exit the baggage area. The next procedure required pushing a button, which activated either a red light or a green one. A red light signified a search of the bags, while a green one meant proceed. I pushed the button, and much to my relief, the light turned green.

Then, to my dismay, I was informed that the luggage cart I was using was not allowed through the security doors. I had to remove my luggage from the cart and drag it through the door into the airport lobby, where, lo and behold, more porters awaited. And people.

A wall of brown faces reminded me that I had just become a minority. Many of those in the happy and excited crowd were waving placards with names on them. I was disappointed to note that none said Ron. Fred, the country manager from Destiny, obviously felt I wouldn't need his help.

I let a porter take my bag and lead me through the throng of people to show me where the money exchange was. Proceeding to the wicket, I exchanged some US dollars for Bolivar's. The exchange rate at the airport was approximately sixty-five (B's as I came to know them), for one US dollar. As frustrated as I was, I still managed to get through the language barrier and accomplish my task. Dick had told me to confirm a price before I got into any taxi. Surrounded by aggressive cab drivers vying for my fare, I picked one, showed him the address and name of hotel where I wanted to go, and negotiated a price.

When I paid the porter, I gave him what I thought was a reasonable amount for his assistance, but in reality had offered him only five cents for his labour. Thus an argument erupted, very one sided, as my tired brain could not decipher the rapid Spanish that was being hurled at me. Annoyed and agitated, I took my bags and put them in the cab, not giving the porter any more for his time. We drove away with the loud cursing of the porter ringing in our ears.

The Maiquetia airport is situated on the Caribbean coast. It was night time and thus a little hard for me to get my bearings as we left the airport. We ascended up from the seaside along on a four-lane highway that was devoid of habitation and lights. The turmoil at the airport left me suspicious of people's motives, so I questioned the driver as to how long it would take us to get into Caracas. The driver did not understand me, so I had to surrender to uncertainty. We progressed steadily upward through numerous tunnels and away from the muggy coastal air. The cool, fresh mountain air slowly extracted the tension from my exhausted body, allowing me to relax and take in my surroundings.

When we arrived on the outskirts of the big city, reality started to hit home. The ghetto on the surrounding hillsides was surreal.

Culture shock began to set in despite my preparations. Resting on the hillsides, one above the other, were thousands upon thousands of tiny shacks. There were no roadways visible, just footpaths up the steep inclines. I wondered how these people managed their water systems, both fresh and waste. And when it rains, what then?

We rounded a corner and the lights of the huge city loomed brilliantly on the horizon. Traffic was light at this time of the morning and before long, we were in the centre of Caracas. Suddenly we left the relatively secure highway and descended into the midst of buildings, travelling on what appeared to be large alleyways. These proved to be main thoroughfares, windy and narrow. I became a little concerned that the cab driver was possibly setting me up, when suddenly 'Hotel Las Americas' loomed up in front of us. I felt an immense sense of relief at the sight of the neon sign glowing forth in the dark back street. In Canada, the small older hotel would not have been very appealing, but here it was a very welcome sight!

I got out, grabbed my bags and proceeded to pay the cab driver. However, there was a problem. He had agreed to one price yet I interpreted another. The argument was on. I thought he had asked for five hundred B's, (about $7.50 US), quinientos. He stated the price was fifteen hundred B's, ($23 US) mil quinientos. I was too tired to argue further, especially with my limited and broken Spanish, so I gave him what he asked for. I later learned that in fact he had been right. The going rate for the forty-five minute ride usually cost about twenty dollars.

Registering at the hotel was the easiest part of the day and I didn't even have a reservation. I asked for a room with hot water and got it. With my passport and plane ticket tucked safely into the hotel safety-deposit box, I headed for my room, finally able to relax. I treated myself to a nice warm shower and then let my weary body collapse onto the bed. I had arrived.

Chapter 3

I AWAKENED IN THE morning refreshed and ready to meet the day. I had my itinerary all planned out. First on the list was to contact Fred at Destiny. Any future action on my part was subject to the directions of my new boss. Once I contacted Fred, I intended to open a bank account and get a safety deposit box. While there, I could also change some currency and get myself orientated in my new world.

However, first things first; it was time for breakfast. The ride in the ancient elevator up to the restaurant was novel for me. I had only seen these odd contraptions in old movies, but I figured out how to operate it, and up I went. An accordion style, metal gate left me diamond shaped openings to observe the concrete wall as I progressed upward.

The restaurant staff were quite accustomed to foreigners staying in their hotel, so when I asked for desayuno americano, they knew more or less what I wanted. It turned out to be a far cry from bacon and eggs, North American style. The bread was thick and slightly toasted. The eggs were greasy and the bacon certainly wasn't crisp. I took a deep breath and said to myself,

"Ron, it's time to start accepting and quit comparing. You're in Venezuela now, not Canada. Look for the good things. Like the orange juice. Certainly don't get it freshly squeezed like this back home."

After the meal, I attempted to phone Fred, but there was no

answer. I decided to step out and see if I could find my way around. Not knowing where the main business area was, this became a hit and miss proposition. I had no map of the city, and as fate would have it, I ventured off in the wrong direction. I soon found myself surrounded by mechanical shops and realized that this was not what I was looking for. I changed direction, and eventually found myself in the center of commerce. Stores, banks and crowds assured me that I had found the right area. I learned that I was on Plaza Sabana Grande. I was immediately overwhelmed by the magnitude of this city with its millions of people, traffic, smells and noises. I was on sensory overload.

I found a bank and tried to open an account. No one spoke English and my broken Spanish made it difficult to communicate. I gave up and went to another bank. I encountered the same situation, and my impatience started to grow. After a third unsuccessful attempt, I decided to take a time-out. I looked around for a place to eat, and was surprised to see a Burger King. At that point, I needed some familiarity more than an adventure in cuisine, so I went inside to have myself a juicy, flame-grilled whopper.

To my dismay, the Burger King was out of hamburger and only had chicken burgers! I could not believe it. I cynically thought to myself, as I stormed out, that they should call themselves Chicken King. I decided if I was going to have chicken, then to a chicken place I should go. I found a Kentucky Fried outlet and they served me some of the best KFC I've ever had. They introduced me to KFC's extra crispy chicken and I immediately became a convert.

I sat outside on the patio savouring the moment and started to take a more relaxed look around. The first thing that caught my eye was how many beautiful women there were; it was as if Venezuela didn't allow anyone on the street who didn't meet up to certain beauty standards. They were dressed immaculately and clean, and when I looked to the hills, I wondered how they could keep their whites so white while living in that squalor. There was just too many of these women; they couldn't all be from the 'good part of town.' Even the men and children were well dressed.

On the Plaza, which consisted of Plaza Venezuela, Plaza Sabana Grande and Plaza Chacaito, there were vendors selling various articles displayed on plywood stands and other such improvisations. The plaza was distinctively designed, laid with brick and trees planted in the boulevard. Vehicles were restricted in this area, which allowed for the flow of pedestrians by the thousands. The sound of horns from the back streets still managed to make its way to my little corner of solitude. This, combined with the salsa music coming from numerous shops, brought a strange chorus of sound to my ears.

I finished my meal and resumed wandering the streets of Caracas. The smells were the next thing to awaken my senses. Ice cream stands invariably had large amounts of their product spilt on the sidewalk, which emitted a very strong, distinct smell. This odour was one I would associate with this place for years to come. As I progressed west, I noticed that there were more vendors and noise. Some of the people I now encountered were poorly dressed and several were dirty and obviously beggars. Nevertheless, they blended in with the normal throng of people. The locals didn't seem to even notice their existence.

A large Banco Union sign enticed me once more inside a bank. I entered and joined the long line up for the teller. We slowly made our way forward. Fifteen minutes later, I stood facing a pleasant young man, a welcome ray of sunshine. His demeanour quickly put me at ease. I attempted to explain to him in my broken Spanish my intent.

"Yo quiero una cuenta del banco."

This was the first time someone actually understood what I was trying to say. After a day of not being able to converse effectively in my new language, this was a refreshing experience. The teller spoke slowly and deliberately, allowing me to comprehend what he was saying. He directed me to a small cubicle where a young lady motioned for me to take a seat. I introduced myself, and again stated my mission.

She started talking rapidly in Spanish. I smiled and pleaded,

"Lento, por favor."

She laughed and asked me, slower this time, if I had an address in Caracas. When I replied that I did not as of yet, she informed me,

"No es possible."

I did not attempt to argue the point. I was exhausted! But I did manage to leave her cubicle with a smile and gracious attitude. I left the bank, a little wiser but with neither an account nor a safety deposit box.

I decided to stop for a coffee at the Gran Cafe, an outside patio that seemed to have a few white faces scattered about. It was quite busy so I quickly found a table and proceeded to people-watch. A waiter passed by and asked me what I would like. I told him,

"Un cafe negro, por favour."

When he returned with a thumb sized plastic cup of pitch-black coffee, I had to refrain myself from laughing aloud. I had a lot to learn. That coffee was so strong I could literally feel the caffeine coursing through my veins.

Noise permeated the air, as music intertwined with car horns, vehicle alarms, people yelling at one another (a local form of conversation I was to discover), and the ever-present sirens from emergency vehicles. The city was definitely alive. Looking about for an ashtray, I noticed that everyone just flicked their ashes on the patio floor. I felt uneasy with this, so I motioned to the waiter by making a butting motion with my cigarette, that I would like an ashtray. He just pointed at the floor. What could I say? When in Venezuela, do as the Venezuelans...

After finishing my cigarette and butting it on the floor, I decided I had better find my way back to the hotel. It was not an easy task. I was hot, tired and my feet were getting sore; all I could do was aim my weary body in the direction of the hotel. I couldn't figure out which street I had come up, so I took a gamble and headed down one that looked likely. The streets ran at all angles and in no time, I found myself lost. I backtracked and tried another way. This continued for about an hour, with me getting more tired, frustrated and worried by the moment. I searched in my pocket and dug out a business card from the hotel. I swallowed my pride, approached a cab driver and showed him the card.

"Donde esta hotel, por favor?"

He graciously pointed me in the right direction and shortly I was back in the safe confines of my temporary 'home.'

I tried calling Fred once more; still there was no answer. Up the rickety elevator and to my room I went, feeling lost, nervous and slightly disorientated. I had noticed that there was a pool and patio on the top floor beside the restaurant, so I donned my swim trunks and immersed myself into the cool water. I floated alone in the pool, letting the day's frustration slowly ebb from my body.

Although I had felt deeply connected with my Higher Power for some time, I was also quite presumptuous of His presence in my daily life. Thus, it seemed He liked to give me a little nudge once in awhile to remind me of His presence. At times, this could be in the form of a set of trials that would finally conclude in my asking for help. The other way was in the form of miracles. Some folks call these coincidences, but in my life, there have been too many of these occurrences to accept that definition anymore. I was about to get one huge 'miraculous' nudge.

As I floated around the small pool, easing my aching body from the day's exertion, I looked up and gasped. There stood Dick, the acquaintance from my hometown. He stood there with big grin on his face, and said,

"What the hell are you doing in there, nobody uses this pool?"

"Why not," I chuckled, as I pulled myself out of the water. Before Dick could answer, I quickly interjected, "Better question, ... what the hell are you doing here?"

"Had to come to Caracas to get a visa for Guyana."

"Well, fancy meeting you here, and is it ever good to see you," I said as Dick led me to a table where another fellow sat.

Dick introduced his companion Albert, who surprised me by speaking clear and concise English. It turned out that he was from Trinidad, but he had lived in Venezuela for many years. The relief of being able to share my day's struggles in English was profound. What a miracle! I didn't even know Dick was in South America, let alone here.

Dick ordered a Cubra Libre, while Albert and I had a Pepsi.

"Why are you going to Guyana?" I asked Dick.

"Going to look at some dredges for mining and see what other possibilities are there," he replied. "Albert has some pretty good connections, so you never know. Chuck and I might get something happening down here." Chuck was a retired road contractor from our hometown and Dick had just retired from a northern underwater diving career. Both men were not quite ready for a life by the pool yet.

We swapped hometown news and other items of common interest until Albert, bored and excluded from the conversation, stated that he had to get home.

"Do you think you could give Ron the grand tour?" Dick asked Albert.

"Be glad to. What time do you want to head out Ron?"

"I'm an early riser, so the sooner the better," I responded.

As Albert left, he stated he would return in the morning and introduce me to the real Caracas. After he left, I returned to my room, changed into clothes and met Dick back on the patio. We had a good meal and passed a very relaxing evening. We agreed to meet in the restaurant for breakfast at about eight. Despite not contacting Fred, nor opening a bank account, the day had ended on a very positive note; meeting a person I know, and the beginning of a long and solid friendship. I didn't know it yet, but in Albert I had met someone who would become a good South American friend and guide. These encounters, neither planned nor prayed for, reassured me that my Spirit Guide was indeed helping me along on my journey.

Chapter 4

THE FIRST RAYS of dawn found me sitting in the restaurant on the top floor of the hotel. From my perch, I could see how Caracas was nestled into the surrounding mountains. There were many high rises, as well as older, more antiquated buildings. From my vantage point, I was able to peer into the daily lives of Caraqueños. There was laundry being hand scrubbed in these little concrete or brick enclosures, then hung up to dry in no precise fashion. The use of clotheslines was obviously not a standard here. There were the ever-present roosters running around and crowing, as well as kids playing or performing some chore. I found myself enthralled by the foreign lifestyle below. My fascination was interrupted by a cheery,

"Buenos Dios!" Dick sauntered up to my table. After an exchange of greetings, Dick stated he would be leaving early to get his visa and then make his way to Guyana. He assured me I would be safe with Albert.

We each had desayuno americano, complete with fresh orange juice, warmed up bread, and now a new drink called guayoyo. This was really just a cup of coffee, but watered down for the benefit of gringos. This word cannot be found in any Spanish/English dictionary and only some places in Caracas understood the term. I was truly grateful to Dick for showing me how to order a decent cup of coffee. We finished our breakfast, said our good-byes, and I was alone again. I resumed watching the inner city life from my lookout,

18

which kept me occupied until Albert showed up.

"Good Morning," said Albert, interrupting my fixation with the life below.

"Hi there, how you doin' this fine day?" I responded.

"Great. You ready to hit the streets for a bit?"

"Let's do it."

So off we went, down the old elevator, and out onto the street. Thus began my three-week education on living and getting around in Caracas. Albert, about thirty-five years old, with a medium build, had a few missing fingers on one hand. My childlike curiosity overrode any subtlety, and I asked,

"So, how'd you lose your fingers?"

"Diving accident. I used to dive for an oil company off shore and got a little tangled up in some cable down below. Had to leave them behind for fish food," Albert replied, with a slight chuckle.

Albert led me back to the plaza that I had discovered the previous day, and proceeded to explain to me the names of the plazas. All one needed to do was look at the names on the Metro stations, accesses to which were centered in each of the three different plazas. He told me that one of the first things he would show me was how to get about on the Metro, the Caracas subway.

We stepped into the subterranean world of the huge city. I was shocked at how clean and organized the subway station was. Even though there were people everywhere, there was a semblance of order. There was no pushing or shoving, and the line up for tickets moved quickly. Albert suggested that I buy a multi-bono ticket, which was good for multiple rides. Once past the wicket, he showed me a map of routes and stops the Metro utilized. I felt disoriented underground and had no sense of direction. With practice though, I would soon get quite proficient at using this very reliable and rapid transit system.

Caracas lay on the south side of a ridge of mountains separating it from the coast. The subway ran parallel to the mountains right through the heart of the city. The Metro (constructed by a French company) was still being expanded. The lack of graffiti and garbage was very noticeable. Quite a change from the streets above! We got on a train heading west and exited one stop later at Plaza Venezuela. I had my wallet in my front right-hand pocket and had a money belt, yet I was still quite leery with all these people swarming around me. This was a pickpocket's paradise. My awareness skills went on full alert as we mounted the stairs to the street above.

We broke into the sunlight, and Albert led me right away to the Gran Cafe, that delightful hub of activity that I had discovered the day before. We sat down and I ordered a "guyoyo grande"; lo and behold, I received a familiar cup coffee. Life was getting better.

"So, how long have you been in Venezuela Albert?"

"Came here from Trinidad about 10 years ago, and have been here more or less ever since."

"What do you do for a living?" I inquired.

"I'm a miner and have several things on the go. Designing a dredge right now, and trying to put some gringos together with some Venezuelans on different mining ventures down in the Grande Sabana," he replied. "And if you're interested, I'll show you some of my ideas later on up at my place."

"Are you married?"

"Oh yes," Albert replied, "in fact I have to go to my place to pick up my daughter shortly. My wife is very involved with her church and that takes up her whole day. I take care of our six-year-old girl when she's not in school. After we finish this coffee we can walk to my place from here, and grab some food for lunch on the way."

We finished our coffee and proceeded west out of the plaza and up a narrow street. There we found a small outdoor fruit and vegetable stand where Albert bought a ripe papaya and a large mango. I trailed along as he entered the adjacent store and bought some sliced meat, unsliced bread and some very strong cheese. The smells placed my olfactory nerve on overload.

We arrived at Albert's apartment building, and now started the agonizing task of sorting through an assortment of keys to gain entry. First, he had to find the key for the main gate, and then the one for the main door. It became my task to hold the food while Albert fumbled with the keys. Once we gained entry to the lobby, we proceeded to the elevator. It resembled the one at the hotel, but the lack of maintenance made this one even more foreboding.

We stepped into the dark, dingy cubicle and locked the mesh door behind us. Albert moved a lever and we shuddered upward. There was no elevator door, which created a strange sensation as we watched the concrete wall pass by. The ride was slow and jerky, but we arrived safely at our floor, opened a gate and exited. We encountered another barred gateway, thus Albert had to fumble for another key. Once through that, one more key put us into his humble abode.

'Wow,' I thought to myself, 'Four keys just to get into his home.'

Then a strange sense of familiarity overcame me. I looked around at all the bar- covered windows and the scene took me back to my old workplace, the gaol. Only now, it felt like I was the one incarcerated. My fear of fire immediately had me concerned, because the only way out was finding those four keys…and quickly.

Albert's' apartment was sparsely decorated. He had minimal furniture but we found a kitchen table and proceeded to build a sandwich from the food we had just purchased. Everything was different for me: the cheese unpasteurized, the fresh bread uncut and the meat had a unique aroma, due to different, yet wondrous spices.

Lisa, Albert's daughter, arrived home from school, and was surprised to find a stranger in her home. But, just like children everywhere, she asked straightforward questions,

"Who are you"? Where do you come from?" and "How do you know my dad?"

This was done in Spanish, as that was her first language. Her mother was from France, so Lisa's second language was French. This bubbly eight-year old quickly assumed the role as my Spanish teacher, and was most unforgiving of my mispronunciations.

Albert got very animated when he pulled out his drawings. His idea of what kind of gold mining dredge he would like to build was his true passion. Of course, having done considerable gold mining myself, he had an attentive audience. Time passed quickly and soon

Lisa got bored, so we decided to go back to the plaza. Before we departed, Albert suggested that I move in with them, and save the cost of living in a hotel.

I said, "I think you better check that out with your wife first."

"I will," he replied.

Once back in the plaza, we strolled leisurely eastward and before I knew it, we were back at my hotel. Albert had to go, but said he would drop by in the morning. After they left, I went up to my room where I encountered another first…a cockroach. A big brute, and since I had never seen one before, it called for another adjustment on my part. Yes, life was truly diverse here. I wanted to experience something different, and at this moment, different was in the form of a six-legged, brown-backed, two-inch long cucaracha!

The following morning Albert returned to the hotel, and together we aimed for his apartment. This time I had an eighty-pound pack on my back. By the time we arrived, I was sweating profusely. There was a mattress on the floor in a spare room, which was where I was to lay my head until I left Caracas. His wife had okay'd this intrusion into her home, as she would not be there much anyway.

The next two and a half weeks were spent learning the ins and outs of Venezuelan life with Albert as my guide, translator, and now, friend. Learning the phone system was one of the first big challenges. Most surprisingly, I noticed that large portions of the population were talking on cell phones. As this was February of 1992, the cell phone craze had not overtaken Canada yet. I soon found out that here, it made real good sense. CANTV was the government phone company, and when a person moved from one residence to another, the phone number stayed with the original establishment, thus the person moving required a new number. This caused many problems when trying to contact people. Moreover, many phone numbers were not of much use after a year or so because of this mobility.

The pay phones mainly operated on phone cards with varying purchase amounts. So when calling long distance to Canada, a larger valued card was required. Then there were good phones, some not so good, others that did not work at all and the odd one that only took coins. Locating good pay phones became of utmost importance. Unfortunately, with good pay phones came long line-ups. When I first arrived, I had used the phone at the hotel. That required going through a Spanish-speaking switchboard and I rapidly discovered that speaking and understanding Spanish on the phone was one of the most difficult issues I was to face.

Finally, I learned how to call Canada direct, eliminating the Spanish operator. I didn't even need to deposit card or coins. I incurred many wrathful looks as I walked up to a pay phone and, without putting in a card or money, pushed some numbers and commenced talking English. The people waiting for the phone couldn't figure out how I avoided the process they had to go through, and on one occasion, a person stepped forth and bluntly asked me how I did that.

My attempts to contact Fred became a daily routine. I contacted Destiny in Canada and they told me that Fred was out in the field with no definite date of return. Although now reassured that my employment was secure, these futile attempts to contact the country manager fuelled my growing anxiety.

Exchanging money for the best rate was another learning curve. Albert brought me to one of the more reputable Cambios (money exchanges) in the area, and they converted my cash for a far better rate than what I could get at the bank. At that time, I could get fifty-five B's for one US dollar. With that, I could buy a package of Marlboro, two or three Pepsis, or five coffees. Everything was cheap when compared to prices back home. Gas in the country was selling for about thirty cents a gallon, so there were cars, motor bikes and buses everywhere. Confident my money would last forever was an illusion that quickly overtook me.

A person making five-hundred B's a day was earning a normal wage. There was a variety of things to buy, clothing being the most popular item on the list. Shoe and clothing stores outnumbered all others and always seemed to be busy. It struck me that these people were enjoying life, and were not overly concerned about the outside world. The fact that they had just endured an attempted coup did not seem to faze them a bit. However, I knew I would need to learn the language better before I could truly qualify that statement.

Albert, Lisa and I visited the park, where there was also a zoo of sorts. Parque Del Este was a very popular spot, where birthday parties abounded and the young ones were beating piñatas to get at the goodies inside. After spending a day in the park, I returned to Albert's place, mentally rested, yet physically drained. I was still acclimatizing, leaving -26°C for these +26 °C temperatures. It was a difficult adjustment, but I certainly wasn't complaining!

About a week after I moved in with Albert, Dick returned to the Las Americas Hotel. I ran into him when I returned to familiar territory for a Pepsi. Another coincidence? I had long sensed that everything happens for a reason and these occurrences substantiated these beliefs. Dick updated me on his latest ventures, and I in turn related mine.

Dick left the next day for Pto. Odaz, and said he would be back in a week or so. I returned to my regular routine, following Albert about, while looking, listening and learning. Finally, after two weeks in country, I made contact with Fred and set up a meeting. I headed over to where he was staying and was shocked by the elegance of the hotel he was at. The Eurobuilding was one of the most expensive hotels in the city, the average room costing two-hundred USD per night. Leather couches, marble floors and gold plated fixtures adorned the lobby. And the receptionist spoke English.

I made my way to Fred's suite and was met at the door by a middle-aged man, six-feet tall, fair skinned, clean-shaven…and unsmiling. His dark, inset eyes emitted an ominous impression that quickly left me feeling very uneasy.

Fred invited me inside and closed the door behind us. As I stood nervously in the foyer, he turned and addressed me in a surly tone.

"Let's cut to the chase," he said, "I never asked to have anyone come down here, nor do I need anyone. So despite what you may have been told by Adrian (the owner of Destiny), I have no position for you here."

"So what exactly am I supposed to do? I just quit my job, spent

my own money getting down here and now you're telling me that
I've been fed a bunch of bullshit! This puts me in quite a position,"
I retorted.

"I told Adrian I didn't need anyone down here. I'm the country
manager here, and decide what I need or don't, so you're going to
have to take this up with Adrian. As far as I'm concerned, there's no
job for you here, and that's that."

"Well, thanks for nothing," I snarled. "And yes, I will be taking
this up with Adrian." And with that, I turned and stormed out the
door. The rage boiling inside me slowly transformed to fear as I
made my way out of the hotel. What was I going to do now? I
jumped into one of the expensive cabs waiting outside and headed
back to the other side of town; dejected, infuriated and alarmed at
the position I now found myself in. I headed to the Gran Cafe to sit
and lick my wounds, trying to figure out my next move.

Up until this trip, daily prayer, meditation and maintaining a di-
ary had been an integral part of my life. Somehow, I forfeited those
practices when I chose to jump into this foreign world. Yet despite
my transgressions, God had not deserted me. He now chose to remind, me in a very big way that He was still watching over me. Time
for another miracle.

Albert showed up with Lisa and I unloaded upon him all my
woes. We left the cafe and headed east down the plaza. We hadn't
walked far, when suddenly I stopped. I pointed my finger ahead and
said to Albert,

"I know those two guys walking towards us; they're from my
home town!"

Sure enough, here in this city of over six million people, I now
encountered two men from Peace River, Maurice, whom I had driven
truck for at one time, and Adrienne whom I had worked with in a
gravel crushing operation. Surprise turned into jubilation as us three
foreigners greeted each other like long lost buddies.

The excitement was contagious; Lisa also found herself in the
fervour of the moment, although she didn't understand what it was
all about. In her enthusiasm, she accidentally bumped the ciga-

rette in my hand and burnt her arm. The joy of the moment was instantly disrupted by her crying and distress. We soon had her calmed, dressed the wound and then we resumed our salutations and introductions.

It was a welcome relief to what had been a very troublesome day. Maurice and Adrienne had just returned from Guyana and were heading home. They wanted to get involved in a mining operation but hadn't found anything worthwhile yet.

Albert now became involved in the conversation.

"I know some people looking for investors down in the Gran Sabana," he said.

"Why don't we go somewhere for supper and talk about it," suggested Maurice.

Over pepper-steak that night, golden opportunities were discussed and dreams enhanced. My life seemed to have prospects again. It was decided that, although they were heading home, Maurice would talk to his brother Chuck, and see what he thought. In addition, Chuck was in constant contact with Dick, so future correspondence would be no problem. My destiny changed that day.

Miracles were abounding in spite my actions. This day, which had started out so negatively, had just taken a turn in a very different direction. My Spirit Guide was obviously working full time on this one, and had certainly received my undivided attention. My humble prayer of thanks that evening was truly heart-felt.

Chapter 5

NOT LONG AFTER my visit with Maurice and Adrienne, Dick returned to the city. He shared our enthusiasm in what we hoped could develop into a gold mining operation. Dick had already been in touch with Chuck who was on a neighbouring island for the winter. Chuck said he would be willing to hop over to Venezuela if there was a substantial reason for him to do so. Entrapped in the concrete jungle, I yearned to break free and head for the Venezuelan rainforest.

As the days progressed, so did my impatience. Carnival was fast approaching, and people told me that a large portion of the population left the city during this period. That sounded good to me. Finally, word came that Chuck was coming over to Venezuela and would meet us in Puerto Odaz. Now we faced a dilemma. How could we get there? All flights to this eastern city were booked solid. My fear of buses ruled out that mode of transportation, as just about every week there was another fatal bus accident somewhere in South America. I suggested to Albert and Dick that we rent a taxi, but they informed me that it was at least a twelve-hour journey and a cab wouldn't be cheap.

I attested, "It can't be that much, let's see what we can find."

Albert replied, "Let me go and check out prices and see if I can find someone willing to leave home this week-end."

We found a 'taxista' willing to forfeit the holiday to drive the four of us across the country for only a hundred dollars! With a great deal of exuberance, we prepared for our departure the following day.

We left Caracas early in the morning, only to find that a person should always be careful what they pray for. On leaving the great city, we discovered that everyone else was doing likewise. So many, in fact, that the police had shut down the two lanes coming into the city, and gave them over to the traffic leaving. Thus we had four lanes of high speed east bound vehicles making the 'great escape.' We found ourselves right in the middle of the madness, speeding along at one-hundred and thirty kilometres an hour in an old 1972 Ford LTD.

The exhaust fumes in the back seat would have overwhelmed me were it not for the fact we could roll down all the windows. As much as I wanted to see the surrounding view, I could not help but do some silent backseat driving…and praying. Sitting up front with the driver, Albert was doing the translating, while Dick sat in the back watching how I was coming to grips with Venezuelan driving. This was just the initialization, as the worst was yet to come.

After about an hour of this four lane mad dash out of Caracas, the highway returned to two lanes in and two lanes out. Soon the highway further diminished to a normal two-lane highway. That was where the fun really began. Our driver had got used to driving at high speeds and was not about to slow down now. The bumper-to-bumper traffic did not intimidate him, as he would pull into the other lane, accelerate, and commence passing as many cars as he could. When coming to a corner, he remained in the wrong lane, despite being blind to what lay ahead. When a semi-trailer truck or other vehicle suddenly confronted us, the cars that we were passing would somehow create a space for us to duck into, thwarting a head-on impact that would have dramatically ended our flight from the city. This not only scared me half to death, it also astounded me that these erratic drivers found some courtesy within themselves to save our situation. This happened repeatedly. Finally, about three hours out of the city, we pulled into a little outside restaurant on the side of the road. I breathed a big sigh of relief.

While the three others ordered a beer with their meal, I had a

Pepsi and settled down enough to take in my surroundings. The first thing I noticed was that the men's urinal was a pony wall, out in the open, and the upper torso of anyone using it was plainly visible to all. In addition, as it was quite dry here, the smell from that area was quite pungent. This destroyed my appetite, so I settled for a soft drink.

"Do you want a beer for the road?" Albert asked the driver in Spanish.

"Si," was the reply.

"Albert, that's all the driver needs. He's crazy as it is," I said in English.

Albert and Dick just laughed, and we crawled back into the 'flying coffin.' The driver did just as I predicted and became more radical than ever. On a positive note, the twelve-hour trip ended in only eight and a half hours, thanks to his driving expertise. When I got out of the car at the Hotel Rasil in Puerto Odaz, I knelt down and kissed the ground, much to everyone's amusement. This was just the first of many harrowing experiences I was to have in this land of Bolivar.

Chuck, a distinguished looking man over six feet tall, lanky and with grey curly hair, was there awaiting our arrival. His relaxed manner helped quell the anxieties that had been building up within me. I had worked for Chuck in the past during my drinking days and our previous affiliation had not ended on a very positive note. My passion for booze overrode common sense, and when I had become a liability, he had made the wise decision to terminate me.

Over drinks in the lounge, a plan was formulated to head south into the gold fields first thing in the morning. Everyone agreed to meet in the lobby at five in the morning, so Albert and I made our way up to the room. I collapsed onto the soft bed with relief and was asleep in a heartbeat.

Much to my surprise, the whole crew was up and ready to go at five as planned. We rode to the airport in a cab, rented a Toyota Land Cruiser, and off we went. The first mistake of the day was letting Albert drive. He was as erratic as the cab driver had been, and I was constantly telling him to slow down.

Not far down the road, we came to our first alcabala (check stop). The Guardia Nacional manned these posts, which I was to learn were commonplace all over the country. The guns and uniform were slightly intimidating, but once we gave them a Spanish newspaper, they waved us on our way.

The carnival was on, and all the different little towns each celebrated in their own manner. We entered the small mining town of El Callao and found that one street had been cordoned off for a parade. This, we discovered, after we had driven down it for about three blocks and the police stopped us. Since we were at an intersection, Albert asked the police officer to let us just proceed ahead around the corner.

The officer responded in Spanish, "You wouldn't drive like this in your country, don't think you can do it here. Back out of here the same way you came in."

Thus, we backed up the three blocks we had come, dodging people, floats and even a few chickens. We made our way out of there and back onto the highway headed south. Soon we entered the dense jungle; this was what I had been waiting for.

We were looking for some mining properties that the artisanal miners were occupying, hand mining without permits, claims or heavy equipment. I was about to step into the past. We made our way up a dirt road heading east until we came to a little mining settlement of tin shacks. One of these "buildings" housed the local grocery store. I attempted to buy a banana, but laughter and teasing by my comrades caused me to rethink this idea. I learned that what I was trying to buy was platano, which has to be cooked to be eaten.

A father and his six-year-old daughter then guided us about their small family operation. I could not believe the amount of work these people did with a shovel, bataya (cone-shaped wooden gold "pan") and a small crusher. These folks lived in a palm-roofed hut, with no walls and slept in hammocks. There were few personal effects visible, yet they seemed to be quite happy. When we were leaving, the young girl came running after us, pointing at me and talking rapidly in Spanish. I did not understand what was going on, until Albert informed me that she really liked my bandana, which I had been wearing about my forehead to keep the sweat out of my eyes. I gladly took it off and gave it to the youngster, who left me with a mental image forever, her running down the path to her home, waving this colourful piece of cloth, as excited as one could be. That turquoise bandana would definitely add some colour to their hut.

We continued up the road until we came to a small trail leading off to the right. Locals told us if we followed it, we would find a small hand mining operation hidden deep in the jungle. Once on this trail, the sky disappeared, and there were only two dominant colours, the red soil of the trail contrasting with the dark green of the jungle. We soon had to resort to walking, as water holes and fallen trees blocked our way. Dick had a good idea of what lay ahead and chose to stay with the vehicle, while Chuck, Albert and I set off on foot into the unknown.

Chuck, who was sixty-three years of age, was a very fast walker, and Albert and I, both a lot younger, had considerable trouble keeping up to him. The trail was not hard to follow, and after two hours of this fast-paced walk, we arrived at the miner's camp. Of course, they were surprised by our intrusion and became defensive. They suspected that we were the claim owners. Albert quickly explained that we were just interested in seeing their operation. These freelance miners soon mellowed out and became quite friendly, taking pride in showing us their meagre holdings. They had a little gas powered crusher set up, which they fed by shovel. This certainly was not a fifty tonne per hour operation.

They invited us to follow them down a footpath deep into the jungle. When we arrived at their site after a half an hour of fast-paced walking, I could not believe my eyes. Here we found a perfectly round hole in the ground, about two meters in diameter and seven meters deep. They had a hand-hewn wooden windlass over the opening that had a rope with knots in it and a bucket attached to the end of the rope. One of the miners shinnied down the rope into the hole, while the other miner passed down a crowbar and shovel for him to work with. Once in the hole, the miner crawled on his belly into a tunnel they had created, a one-meter square opening underground that ran horizontally following a gold-bearing quartz vein. The use of any shoring or timbers to hold up this structure did not appear to be of any consequence to them. They told me that the tunnel went in about ten meters.

This quartz was very rotten, and crumbled quite easily. The miner proceeded to mole out some gold-bearing material, while we waited and looked around. Once he had enough to fill the bucket, the other miner hoisted it up, while the other fellow climbed out of the hole using the knots on the rope and some footholds cut into the wall of the pit. The miner hoisted the sack of gold ore onto his shoulders and led us back to camp. I struggled to keep up, even though he stood only about five and half feet tall, and had over one hundred pounds on his back!

We arrived back at the camp and the miners proceeded to feed the material into their little crusher. Once crushed, the material was placed in a heavy, hand carved wooden bataya, which one of the miners submersed in the creek. Bent over and taking the primitive gold pan in both hands, he manoeuvred the full pan in a circular motion. This caused the heavier substances to go to the bottom, allowing for the discarding of the valueless rocks and dirt that remained on top. He then added some mercury that quickly absorbed the gold within. I wasn't prepared for what he did next!

The miner took the mercury conglomerate from the bataya, curled up his shirttail, and placed the quicksilver in it. He then wrung the shirt tight and squeezed the water and some mercury through the cloth. What remained in his shirttail was a gold-laced hard piece of mercury. With a large grin, the miner strutted toward the hut with his prize, and lit the propane stove within. He took a large spoon, put the mercury/gold piece in it and placed it over the fire. All of this transpired within the confines of the wall-less hut! I had once received a dose of the toxic mercury into my lungs and I knew how dangerous this process could be. One small whiff and I had been sick for three days. These people were working with this dangerous substance inside a hut with no wind present to blow these fumes away. This was crazy and I made sure I stayed well back until the mercury was burned off.

And then, there it was; that allusive yellow material that these men had toiled for was now shining brilliantly forth from the spoon. In this first round, their reward was about two grams of gold, or about twenty dollars. This they would split four ways, and of course, there were supplies and food to purchase. Anyone thinking that this was easy money ought to try filling a Venezuelan miner's sandals for a day. I now received a glimpse of what it must have been like in the Yukon gold rush so long ago. The one big difference here was the lack of severe cold, but the primitive living and working conditions must have been quite similar.

We thanked the men, and headed back to the vehicle. We had been gone approximately four hours and Chuck was anxious to get back.

"Chuck, you walk a lot faster than me. Dick is going to be getting worried, so why don't you go ahead and Albert and I will take up the rear?"

"Okay, but I'll carry the video camera to make it easier for you," Chuck said.

In no time at all our partner was out of sight; Albert and I were left alone plodding through the jungle. We came to a fork in the trail and I was sure that our path lay to the right, while Albert insisted the main trail was straight ahead. Since he had more experience in these settings, I followed him. However, after a half an hour of not seeing anything familiar and arguing with Albert, I sat down.

"I'm not going any further. We're on the wrong trail."

"No, I'm sure this is the right one," retorted Albert.

Albert (stubborn to the core), proceeded on down the trail while I sat and watched some ants. They had worn a trail in the soft ground and marched purposefully in one direction. Occasionally, one would attempt to go the opposite way. The big black insects would then block his way and turn him around. Right now, Albert was much like that wayward ant.

It was getting late and I realized that there was a real possibility I could end up spending the night in this forbidding spot. I turned my focus to the various plant forms and vines that surrounded me. My mind started to construct a hammock out of them, as I did not relish the idea of sleeping on the ground with all the insects and reptiles.

I kept vocal contact with Albert, and when he could barely hear me anymore, he reluctantly admitted his error and returned. Now we had to backtrack and take up the trail again. We arrived back at the vehicle about fifteen minutes before dark, and were greeted by the concerned faces of Dick and Chuck. They had not known what course of action to take if we had not returned before nightfall. My very first voyage into the tropical jungle, and I had come very close to spending a night in it. It was some time before I forgave Albert for that experience.

Back on the road towards town, Albert stopped the vehicle to let a large, furry tarantula make his way to the other side of the road. The sight of that formidable insect crawling back into the jungle enhanced my gratitude for the safe confines of the vehicle. We arrived in Tumeremo at about nine in the evening, and with the carnival on, there were no rooms available. After trying numerous hotels, we finally found an abysmal one for five dollars a night. Tired after the days exertion, I didn't care what the room was like, I just wanted to crash.

I dragged myself to my meagre room, and found my shower facility consisted of a forty-five gallon drum full of water and a metal dipper. I took the ladle and proceeded to splash water over my tired torso. After that was accomplished, I dried myself off and fell into bed.

I had barely fallen asleep, when I was abruptly awakened by the sensation of fire all over my body. I jumped out of bed and discovered fire ants all over my torso. I ran to the drum of water, grabbed the dipper and started splashing them off. What a rude awakening! Now what? My bed, now infested with these little red demons, was no longer an option. I was dead tired and desperately needed rest.

Therefore, I curled up in a corner of the cement floor and soon fell asleep, putting closure on this first day's excursion into the jungles of South America.

Chapter 6

L ITTLE DID I know but my 'Spanish lessons' would be taken to a whole new level, taking on more than one connotation. I had observed on our arrival in Pto Odaz, that there seemed to be a multitude of attractive women about the hotel. This first evening on my own, I concluded that the time had come for me to acquaint myself with one of these beauties. To do so would require entering the lounge, a proposition that caused me some hesitation. After all, it was a 'slippery' place, potentially dangerous to my sobriety. To consume even one drop of alcohol would launch me onto a course that could only end with me in dire straights, as my personal history could attest. Refortifying myself with a little self-talk, I said a prayer and wandered inside.

Taking a second or two for my eyes to adjust to the dim lighting, I found my way to the bar, greeted the bartender and straddled a barstool. It had been many years since I had frequented an establishment such as this alone. However, I was not to be solo for long. Before I had a chance to order a Coke, a lovely lady sat down at my side, and asked me for a light.

As I held the lighter to her cigarette, she peered over the flame into my eyes, and with a sensuous smile, asked, "Un bebito para mi, por favor."

I nodded my head to the bartender, and then inquired, "Como su nombre?

She told me her name was Lia, asked me mine and thus began

my lessons in Castellano. Now came time for the trusty old pocket translator. Lia had a good sense of humour and the two of us hit it off right away, using the translator constantly.

"Cuantos años tiene?" I asked.

"Treinta y dos." she responded.

Lia did not look anywhere near the thirty-two years of age she claimed to be, stunningly attractive and emitting a youthful exuberance. She had short black hair and big brown eyes and a body that filled her black slacks and red blouse quite agreeably. Her friendly manner put me at ease and when her hand rested on my thigh, I was quite grateful once more to have some gentle female contact. Lia had a contagious laugh and soon had Miguel (the bartender) and myself in stitches as she tried mastering a few words in English.

The process was simple: she would type a word into the translator in Spanish, press enter and attempt the English pronunciation, which was usually followed by an eruption of laughter. Then, I tried certain Castellano translations, eliciting the same reactions. This went on for hours. The laughter felt good, the female company invigorating and I started to unwind from the preceding days of worry and excitement.

I was thoroughly enjoying the Latin music. Diveana was popular at the time, and her music was very upbeat. There was as well, a good mixture of merangue and salsa. Other women would join us for a while, until another prospective male entered the lounge. Then off they would go to share their companionship with the new arrival. I continued buying Lia drinks and she seemed to hold her liquor quite well.

She had one friend, a tall woman with long, pitch-black hair, whose name was Juanita. She was striking as she strode across the room, her height being out of the ordinary here. Juanita joined in the laughter and tried her hand with the translator. These two women kept insisting that I get up and learn how to salsa, but that was a little more than this cowboy could handle on his first night out.

I was enjoying the moment, the dim glow of red backlights enhancing the overall ambience. I was captivated by Lia's sensuality.

She wasn't shy. Her eyes were mischievous and she had a way of making overt sexual innuendos out of the slightest opportunity. Thus, after about five hours of flirting, I felt the time had come to challenge these covert suggestions and invited her to my room. A smile spread across her lips as she leaned over and whispered in my ear,

"Vamanos," the Spanish interpretation for 'let's go'.

Once in my room, neither one of us had any inhibitions, nor did we waste any time quelling our passions. Some time later, I fell into a blissful sleep, more relaxed than I had been in a long, long time.

In the morning, as Lia was getting ready to go home, she mentioned that her son needed some dental work. Catching the hint, I gave her about fifty dollars, and she was gone. A whole evening of unhurried companionship was worth that and much more.

I went for breakfast, and had just sat down, when a lovely young Columbian woman approached my table and asked if she could join me. I must have shown my surprise, because she quickly explained that she had just come into town, travelling all the way from Columbia. New to the scene, she was as uninformed and as naive as I was. Therefore, I bought her breakfast and I could not help but gaze at this exquisite Columbiana. She was petite, with sharp facial features and gorgeous emerald green eyes. Her smile would melt an iceberg, and I felt myself filling with desire for this luscious Latina. She subtly implied that she would like to spend some time with me, and before I knew it, we were in my room. This rendezvous was a little more formal, and she asked for some financial help, for which I quickly obliged. And then she was gone.

I felt like a kid left alone in a candy store. My male hormones were flowing, and my virility was being tested. I felt about fifteen years younger, life was good and my old adage came into play, "If it feels good, do it!"

I then retired to the poolside where I met Jack, an American employed installing a pipeline across the Orinoco River. He set about enlightening me on what was transpiring in this very affluent Venezuelan city.

"Pto. Odaz is on the western side of the Caroni River, while San Felix is on the other. The two cities combined share the name Ciudad Guyana. On the eastern half of the city in San Felix, live the working poor, and over there the living conditions are quite bleak. Here in Pto. Odaz, live the upper middle class and rich, so you won't see any slums," he said.

It became apparent why so many beautiful women were all about. They had come to exploit the men, rich ones or those they deemed so. I fell into this latter category. The perception that a "gringo" equated to money pervaded every part of society, and this place was no exception. These women, here of their own volition, came not only from all over Venezuela, but also neighbouring Columbia, Brazil and Guyana. Money and a good time were their primary incentives.

"Beware," Jack exclaimed warningly, "More than one of my buddies has gone home broke."

A young Brazilian woman soon joined us, drinks were bought and more good-natured joshing and banter ensued. Soon I was in the pool frolicking with this beauty in my newfound paradise. Then I looked up and there on the balcony stood Lia. She wasn't smiling. I chose to ignore her, but the Brasilera didn't. Intimidated by the scowl from above, my new companion told me she had to go, left the pool and disappeared. I returned to my table with Jack, and we continued our conversation. After some time, I returned to my room for a siesta.

That evening I returned to the lounge, wanting to encounter more of these southern delights. It wasn't long before I had Lia back at my side. We took up where we had left off and I soon realized that, be what these women may, they were also very possessive. I was her catch! Moreover, since she had been around the scene for a while, the other girls were not about to mess around in her domain. I resigned to life with Lia, the less complicated option for the moment. Besides, it appeared I had the best company of the lot. Thus Lia became my partner, guide and Spanish teacher for the duration of my first visit to Pto. Odaz.

The pleasant part of these unique relationships was the absence of financial negotiation. Conducted in the fashion that it was, both the women and the men could maintain their dignity. Proper or not, I had entered a very sensual world where desires were satisfied and everyone gained. Social mores be damned! These women enjoyed not only the money, but also what they did to earn it. Many evenings were spent in conversation where drinks were bought and Spanish lessons served. The girls received a certain amount of money for every drink purchased, so they did not need to do anything else if they did not want to. I was a real oddity to them in that I only drank Coke or Pepsi, and of course, that did not help their coffers. Nevertheless, they soon learned that my sobriety could not be compromised.

I was continually aware of how much I was flirting with the devil by placing myself in close proximity to my insidious old enemy, alcohol. I asked Lia to try to find a twelve-step meeting for me somewhere, to which she promptly agreed.

For the next couple of weeks, Lia guided me downtown, to the park, zoo and other sites. I came to know the area quite well. At the zoo, I had my first encounter with an irate, chattering monkey. I swatted him with a newspaper for getting too close and he proceeded to chase me up the trail. As I threw rocks back at the irate primate, I found myself reassessing my opinion of cute little monkeys.

Around eleven o'clock one evening, I took Lia out for supper at a nice open-air steak house. Good eating establishments didn't open until after seven pm and most people dined at about nine pm or so. We were eating our meal when this little waif came in who appeared to be about five years old. The waiter immediately went to whisk him out, but Lia grabbed the little boy and told the waiter to leave him with us. This child was dirty with matted hair and had a very sad and tired face. He was hungry so we shared some of our meal with him, although he could barely keep his eyes open. As he sat on Lia's knee, she queried him on what he was doing out at this time of night, where his mother was and his age. It turned out that this lad was eight years old and out begging money. This was very strange because in this part of the city there was virtually no poverty. The only thing that we could surmise was that his mother must have been a drug user and had sent him out to obtain money for her. It was very heart breaking, and although we both wanted to take this child home, clean him up and let him sleep, we knew we couldn't do that. He fell asleep in Lia's lap. When it was time to go, we awakened the toddler and sent him on his way. I had just been jolted into one of the realities of my new surroundings.

One evening, Lia informed me that she had found a meeting and asked if she could accompany me. She said she was tired of her own constant drinking but did not know how to get out of the vicious cycle that her life had become. That night we both set off for our first Venezuelan meeting.

We soon found an abandoned house that had been turned into a meeting place. An enthusiastic group of people quickly greeted us, and I rapidly felt the familiarity I had been missing. This was like home away from home. Even though everyone spoke Spanish, they also spoke the universal language of the heart, which had saved my life so many years ago.

After a two-hour meeting for which I was sure Lia would be upset, I was shocked when she asked why I hadn't told her about this before. The group offered her hope and encouragement in a way she had never known. She readily accepted the pathway to recovery, and the lounge lost a regular source of income from that night forward.

I returned to that hotel some years later and enquired of Miguel about Lia. He told me that she had moved to another town and had opened the dress shop she had always dreamed of. And yes, she had stayed sober. Sadly, things had not turned out as well for Lia's friend. Juanita had committed suicide.

Dick called from Caracas and asked me if I wanted to go to Guyana. He wanted to fly over there to look at a gold dredge that was for sale. I jumped at this opportunity and told him I would take a plane and be in Caracas the following morning. Time for play was over and none too soon, as my finances were quickly depleting.

Chapter 7

"Ron, I'm telling you now, be prepared for culture shock. What you see here is nothing like over there. You think Caracas is a city in a third world country, but Venezuela is in fact a developing nation. Guyana is a third world country." Dick's ominous description proved to be an understatement.

Well warned, we boarded the plane for Georgetown, and off we flew. It seemed like we were over the mouth of the Orinoco River for hours. An immense expanse of sand coloured water flowed below us, threading its way through numerous islands and ultimately pouring itself into the Caribbean; the long journey from the Amazon jungle concluded.

The plane landed at the International Airport, which lay south of the city of Georgetown. Assailed by the humidity, I had to stop and grab the handrails as I stepped down from the plane. Regaining my composure, I made my way down the ramp and into the yellow clapboard building that served as a terminal. There was a big red line with a large sign informing passengers not to cross it until called. No vending machines or other such conveniences here. Once a British Colony, some of that old stiff regimen was still very apparent. We finally made it through customs and stepped outside, again confronting the stifling heat and humidity. Dick made a deal with a cab driver and we headed for his car. I opened the right-hand door and was shocked to see a steering wheel there. I looked over my shoulder to see Dick and the cab driver having a real good laugh at my expense.

"They drive on the wrong side here," Dick said laughing.

The drive into town was bizarre to say the least, with us driving on the left hand side of the road, dodging cows, chickens, donkeys and a variety of other animals wandering across the highway. Chickens were everywhere. So were Ford tractors. People were using them as personal vehicles as well as work machines. Men, women and children adorned the fenders and hoods of these big blue machines, while other tractors were pulling carts full of people, animals or household items.

Houses were mounted on stilts and constructed with boards that had not seen paint in years. Dick had been right, this place was far different than I could ever have imagined. As we dodged the road obstacles, the sense of poverty was overwhelming. It was everywhere. Nothing seemed to be maintained at all. Most noticeable was the lack of smiles on the faces of those persons we passed. The real gauge of poverty is not the lack of material trappings; it is the absence of joy.

An interesting half-hour drive from the airport had us in the center of Georgetown. Here, the majority of buildings were constructed of clapboard lumber rather than concrete. Some were nicely painted and stately, while the vast majority were rundown and weathered. We arrived at our hotel, checked in and made our way to our respective rooms. I was sweating profusely by this time, as the climate was oppressive. I changed quickly into my swim gear, dove into the pool and I slowly regained my composure.

After I had cooled down, I exited the pool taking a seat at a table on the adjacent patio. No sooner had I sat down, when two pretty, young women joined me at my table.

One of them asked, "You're a friend of Bob, right?"

"Who's Bob?" I responded.

She apologized for mistaking me for someone else and then asked me if I would buy them both a drink. This odd way of introducing themselves was quite different from what I was accustomed to. I had not even been in the country for two hours and there I sat with two gorgeous women who spoke English. They were obviously of East Indian descent, very small in stature, and my guess was that they were both in their mid twenties. The smaller one introduced herself as Sasha, while the other woman had a name I couldn't pronounce. They were both dressed quite casually, wearing white blouses and medium length black skirts. Their attire did not bespeak anything other than two normal, middle class women.

They commenced talking between themselves in a different form of English, one that I could not decipher. After their exchange, Sasha turned to me and stated in very clear English, "My friend has to go, but I can stay for awhile. Where are you from?"

"Canada," I replied.

"I thought so. There have been many Canadians down here lately. Are you a gold miner?" she asked.

"I'm a 'wanna be'," I replied.

Sasha then started steering the conversation with sexual innuendos and flirting with her deep, dark eyes. It was only four in the afternoon and I was still adjusting to this major change of climate and scenery. I got a bit defensive with Sasha, not fully comprehending what was going on. She didn't look at all like a girl working the sex trade, yet her advances were quite blatant. I soon relaxed, let nature take its course and within three hours of entering the country, I found myself in the embrace of this lovely Guyanese woman.

In the course of the next few hours, I plied her with questions. What her motive was for pursuing this total stranger was the first thing I wanted to know.

Slowly, as she unveiled what life was like in this remote part of the world, it all began to make sense. Guyana was now the poorest country in South America, thus Sasha's infatuation with me. I could be her ticket out of there.

Sasha informed me that she was a registered nurse, had trained in Haiti and currently made a dollar twenty-five a day working at the local hospital. Her job entailed working with AIDS patients in a special ward that had been set up to deal with this local epidemic. She claimed that there were about forty people housed in that unit, but far more than that had just walked out and blended back into the community, no longer seeking medical attention. The population of the whole country was about 750,000 people, so this presented a very precarious situation. Such statistics were a loud wake up call for this vagabond.

Dick finally arose from his siesta, and joined us for supper by the pool. It was very difficult to hold a conversation due to the drone of cicadas coming from a large tree in the courtyard. This noise continued resonating non-stop. Since it was hard to converse, Sasha decided to go, but she promised to drop by the next day. I retired to my room, alone this time, and lay there reflecting on this strange land and its diverse occupants.

The following day we set about trying to set up viewing a dredge that was for sale. Dick had talked to the owner on his previous visit, taking care of preliminaries such as transport to the mining site. The owner, one of the richest people in the city, had three of these large gold dredges working on the Potari River. He offered us his airplane and pilot to fly us into the jungle. He could not accompany us, as he was a race car driver and had pre-trials that day.

Dick and I made our way to a small airstrip located within the city. There we found the pilot and his craft, a Cessna 206, mounted on floats. The floats had wheels mounted on them that would allow us to take off from this land-based strip.

The pilot, Dick and I got in, taxied down the concrete runway, and off we flew. My aerial view of Georgetown was brief as we were soon soaring over the immense jungle canopy. As we followed the wide Esquibo River south, I gazed at the numerous rapids on this mighty river and wondered how we could ever navigate a large dredge through those treacherous waters to the coast.

When we turned southwest, the river disappeared and we found ourselves flying over an expanse of green foliage that spread to the horizon in every direction as far as the eye could see. We flew over a circular clearing that contained a cluster of cone shaped thatch huts. I could see no water source from our vantage point, so I questioned the pilot.

"That is triple canopy jungle down there and there are small rivers. You just can't see most of them," he replied.

Not long after he said that, than the serene scene below was shattered. The incursion of dredges had left the virgin landscape below scarred with piles of sand and fallen trees. The small river below us widened, and was dotted with the dredges that we had come to see. They were busy chewing their way into the banks, causing huge trees, foliage and probably the odd reptile to topple into the muddy water.

We landed on the river, taxied up to one of the dredges and stepped out onto the pontoons. Once more, the humidity hit me with a blast. We made our way onto the dredge, introductions were completed and then the leader of the crew began to show us his operation.

This gold mining apparatus consisted of a pair of pontoons about forty feet in length and twenty feet wide. The sluice was mounted on one end, extending for about fifteen feet and covering the whole width. To catch the gold, pieces of angle iron were placed strategically on top of green outdoor carpet that lay the full length of the sluice. The other end of the dredge had the motor and a large water pump. A ten-inch suction hose hung suspended from an A-frame apparatus mounted on a small pontoon in front of the dredge. A winch was used to send the hose down to the riverbed to suck up the gold bearing gravel. The water and gravel then gushed into a large metal hopper, filled with baffles to direct the flow evenly across the width of the sluice. When things ran smoothly, the flow of material came through at a rate of about 250 cubic meters of gravel in a twelve-hour shift. With this fusion came about 1450 cubic meters of water, thus there was a lot of material running over that sluice in the course of a day. Every gold-miner knows there are good recoveries and bad. These miners proudly exclaimed that the pay-dirt here averaged three ounces of gold per hour. Poor production was not discussed.

A tin roof covered the full length of the dredge, for this was also the living quarters for this crew of four. They slung their hammocks wherever they could and had a small propane stove set up by the motor where they prepared their meals. This was rustic living at its finest. Nature calls were done over the side of the dredge and all drinking water was boiled. The water was heavily polluted from all the mining activity and boiling the water did nothing to get rid of all the mercury, which was residual from the various gold cleanup operations.

When we arrived, two of the miners were wading in thick, brown water, wrestling with a tree stump that had fallen into their little pond. Dealing with these monstrous trees was a chore in itself. The men worked without chainsaws, relying on brute force and machetes to wrestle these obstacles out of the way. As I watched these men working in that mire, I couldn't help but wonder how many wild critters, such as snakes and piranha might be amongst them.

We finished our tour, got our information and boarded the plane. Our take off from that small river was nerve racking. We had to dodge floating debris, skim around a corner and not scrape along any gravel bars. The added weight of the gold we had just picked up didn't help matters. The smile on the southern bush pilot's face said it all; he revelled in this opportunity to display his expertise.

Once back in civilization, we landed at the International Airport and taxied over to the racetrack, which just happened to be adjacent to the airport. We stepped out of the plane and walked directly to the race car pit to talk with the benefactor of our adventurous day. I was still reeling from the whirlwind ride. In just a few short hours, we had flown from the center of town out over miles of jungle, landed on a river, picked up several kilos of gold, returned, landed on another concrete airstrip and taxied directly to a race car track.

The rest of the week was spent dealing with the logistics of moving the proposed dredge from Guyana into Venezuela. I met with the captain of a ship that hauled Bauxite directly into Pto. Odaz. He agreed to have the disassembled dredge placed on his upper deck. All this, of course, for a price. We then met with government agencies to find out what was involved in exporting this equipment, and in the course of it all, I got a chance to feel the heart of Georgetown.

The first thing I observed was that it was not a safe place like Venezuela. Anytime I left the hotel, I had a taxi driver/bodyguard with me, even in the middle of the day. Such caution was not unwarranted. In the course of one day, while I was in this very small city, one person was kidnapped, another murdered and I observed a maniac run down the sidewalk brandishing a bicycle as a battering ram, knocking down anyone who was in his way.

Sasha continued to join me poolside, sharing with me the many customs and ways of this English speaking South American country.

The remnants of affluent days long past were clearly visible everywhere. Abandoned buses, vehicles and equipment sat rusting away alongside majestic old buildings slowly deteriorating from lack of paint and care. All this sadly reflected the equal state of the population, or at least a large portion of it.

The stench of poverty was everywhere. Sewage, rotting dead animals and other grotesque smells assailed my nostrils. The ocean was filthy thanks to two large rivers depositing their silt, sewage and murky water there. I could not imagine anyone swimming in this slime, yet I did see young children playing on the beach.

One day, three young boys, who were begging for money, accosted me on the street. These street urchins had no shoes, were dirty and had tangled long hair. I reached into my pocket, took out some change and gave each one a coin. To me it was nothing, but the boys immediately started fighting with each other. It turned out I had given them all different amounts. I quickly fled the scene, but encountered them some hours later, all bruised and battered. They again wanted money but this time they left empty handed.

Back at the hotel, Dick insisted I see the market. To this day, I have never entered a market that comes close to that one for overwhelming the senses. When we arrived, a man was transporting some raw meat in a wheelbarrow engulfed with a horde of flies. Inside the complex, the odour of raw fish mingled with the smell of curry. Spices, incense, fish and the ever-present pungent stench of rotting meat all lent their scents to form a bizarre potpourri of odour.

There were, however, some very positive aspects to the market. I was fascinated by the colourful scarves and cloth on display by the East Indian culture, as well as the carpets and other hand-stitched wares. But the most awe-inspiring of all was the work exhibited by the goldsmiths. The pride in their workmanship was well deserved. Intricate designs and minute detail were apparent in nearly all of their jewellery. Most astonishing of all was the price they charged for their artisanship. Many of these items could be bought for just slightly more than the present rate of pure, uncrafted gold. Dick was right. The market on the Esquibo was definitely an experience not soon forgotten.

Another interesting observation was that, for the most part, the East Indian people owned the majority of the businesses and were the most affluent. Their counterparts, the black citizenry, were the politicians, police, the very poor and a large portion of the criminal element. The animosity between the two sects was prevalent everywhere.

We changed money in the backroom of a textile fabric shop and the Guyanese dollars were placed in a paper bag – a big bag. It took many bills to make the equivalent of one-hundred American dollars when the exchange was about two-hundred Guyanese dollars for one US dollar. The banks did not offer a fair exchange rate and their operating hours were minimal. While we conducted this money exchange, unsavoury characters stood outside watching and waiting for a chance to grab our bags of cash. Fortunately, with help from the money vendors and our bodyguards, we managed to thwart their vile plans.

A week after arriving we departed. I was slowly becoming a little more travel savvy. One thing that surprised me was my ignorance of the world outside of my own. As I reflected on all those in poverty through no fault of their own, the desire to rescue Sasha from the squalor she lived in, or to whisk the children off the streets and get them back into school, flooded my conscience. It was with a heavy feeling in my chest that I realized I could not save the world.

What I could do though, was become more aware of situations that presented me with an opportunity to spread some hope, help or charity. I would have to be vigilant against becoming hardened by such immense oppression, and for that to happen, it would be necessary to keep an open heart and mind.

Chapter 8

NOW THAT SOME of the logistics had been arranged, the key to the whole venture now rested on acquiring the right to work with a dredge on the Rio Caroni. The construction of a power dam was about to cause the area to flood, creating a man-made lake. Very soon, tons of gold were going to be far out of reach below its surface. The miners had done a thorough job of sifting through the gravel bed on the bottom of the river, but had recently discovered that they had only been touching the surface of a hard crust on the river bottom. Once the crust was pierced, the miners had access to a completely new layer of rich gold-bearing gravels. New types of dredges with cutting edges and 'missiles' had been developed to allow for the extraction of this new material. Time was of the essence.

Albert started making some necessary contacts. This was going to require people with connections to facilitate our goals. Of course, money greases the bureaucratic wheel, thus we did what was necessary. However, nothing happens fast in Venezuela, so I headed back to Pto. Odaz where my impatience could be tempered by the glamorous distractions that abounded there.

By this time, Chuck was getting ready to head to the Yukon. He had been successfully gold mining there for several years and had a lot of preparation to do for the busy season ahead.

Chuck had started to have some faith in me by this time, seeing that I was staying sober and the Ron of old had not emerged.

Therefore, he let me know that if the Venezuelan project did materialize, I would be included in the team. For the time being, he requested that I remain available to take care of any logistics that may arise. He also advised me that if things didn't work out, he could put me to work in the Yukon if I was interested. That was good enough for me. I now had a plan A as well as a plan B. Life was good!

Back in the city of my dreams, I took up where I had left off, this time free from the restrictions I felt when Lia was around. I spent days by the pool and evenings in the lounge pursuing my "Spanish lessons." My Spanish was improving immensely and becoming beneficial. While on the plane back to Pto. Odaz, I was able to listen in on a conversation two Venezuelan men were having. They were discussing their pursuit of the same objective we were after. This helped me put things in their true perspective. We had competition from people with far more experience and connections than we had, all scrambling for the same goal. (I found out later that there were only 63 of those concessions released, and they did not even get to work the full five years originally projected, as the dam was in place and water backed up far sooner than expected).

I was enjoying life to the fullest, but it didn't come cheap. As my funds slowly ebbed away, so did time. I was becoming very familiar with one of the most used words in the Spanish language, mañana, which literally meant tomorrow (but figuratively meant whenever). Habit had me interpreting the precise meaning of the word most the time, which caused many disappointments. I soon found myself getting into an uncomfortable financial position.

There finally came a time when I had to admit defeat and start preparing for a return to Canada. That was going to be one huge ego deflation. I had left with such great fan fare and high aspirations. The depleted bank account finally helped me make the regretful decision. I had spent most of my pension money, as well as the cash from my material liquidation. I could not help but hear the distant echo of Jack's words, "Beware." He had warned me how astute the women here were at parting men from their money. I never had been too smart at taking sound advice.

A call to Chuck confirmed I had a good paying job waiting for me the Yukon. I also had another good piece of fortune. I salvaged my pickup truck that had failed to sell while on consignment. Formerly distressed about it not selling, I was once more reassured that everything happens for a reason.

My taste for adventure whetted, I was certain I would return; one way or the other. After all, I was hooked on a drumbeat!

Humbly, I returned to Canada. Fortunately, my twelve-step friends held no judgement on me as they helped me swallow my pride and refortify my spirit. Family, as always, was supportive and relieved to see me back home. They no doubt felt that I had quelled the deep urge for adventure and would now settle down.

However, I did not linger long in Peace River. I drove north up the Alaska Highway and soon found myself in temperatures well below zero Celsius, a vast difference from the average twenty-seven degrees Celsius I had become accustomed to. I found solace in the pristine landscape unfolding before me, still blanketed in pure-white snow. Close to Dawson City, I headed south off the beaten trail and ventured into a world devoid of habitation.

It was early in the year, so most of the regular miners had not arrived yet. The drive into the mine was about one hundred and sixty kilometres. I guided my 4x4 over three mountain ranges and three ice-covered rivers. Throughout this journey, I did not meet or see one vehicle. From the noise and hustle bustle of Latin America, to the quiet solitude of the Yukon, this was an extreme change, even for me. The excitement of four-wheeling through this magnificent wilderness soon obscured any feelings of disappointment lingering from my last endeavour.

Once I arrived at the camp, I immediately commenced operating a D-8 cat doing preparatory work with settling ponds. It felt great to be gainfully employed once more. We tore up the frozen ground with Caterpillar D-9 tractors and moved the dirt to the side. This gave us access to the gold bearing material hidden beneath. We ripped this gravel up and laid it to thaw in the sun in preparation for sluicing. We worked seven days a week, twelve hours a day. This suited me fine, as we ate good and had a nice camp. I formed some new friendships, yet preferred the solitude I found while exploring the surrounding area during my free time.

From time to time, someone had to go to town for food and parts. I was privileged to make many of these trips which could take anywhere from five to eighteen hours depending on the condition of the road. Many times, I contemplated starting an 'Extreme Tours' business, conveying thrill-seekers on these expeditions. One personal benefit of these trips was a chance for me to get to twelve-step meetings while in town. I was very grateful to have that sincere kinship in this remote northern community.

Two members of our crew conducted a trip, which I was fortunate enough not to make. They lost their brakes descending a steep hill and had to jump from the truck, which careened over a cliff and was completely demolished. This left one of them still capable of walking, while the other two (one being a miner they had picked up on the way) were severely injured. Fortunately, there was a mining camp close by with a radio to call for help. A helicopter arrived and flew the injured men out to civilization. One of them required medical treatment in Edmonton, while the other was treated locally. Miraculously, no one sustained permanent injuries.

On another occasion, these same two men tried crossing a river at night and the truck was swept into a big hole. Water was soon flowing through the cab, entering through the passenger side window and exiting out the driver's window. Both men had to crawl out of the window onto the top of the vehicles canopy from where they were able to make their way to shore. Again, fortune blessed them, as there was a mining camp nearby. I was sent looking for them the next day and found I couldn't cross the river in the normal place. I followed the shore upstream and then entered the fast-flowing river, driving and bobbing downstream diagonally to the other side. This traverse was a hair-raising experience with force of the swift river propelling me downstream.

A friendly neighbour had pulled their truck from the river with a front-end loader. I found the weary travellers attempting to dry out the inside of their truck. All oils had to be changed and the damage to the electrical system was extreme. One fellow returned with me while the other remained behind to try to repair his vehicle. By the time we reached the river, the water level had dropped considerably. This time the river was kind.

We started sluicing at the beginning of June, when the material we had exposed had finally thawed and the ice was gone from the river. We had a very successful summer, producing a large amount of the precious yellow substance. This stimulated me to go searching for some of my own, so I started exploring in my free time. I found an old dredge, complete with rusty sluice runs and even manila matting used to catch the gold. Days in the north were now long, with the sun barely setting. I could pan to my hearts content in the Land of the Midnight Sun.

One such night, I was to experience something that I had heard of, but until this occasion, had never experienced – Gold Fever! While diligently panning material found in the bottom of the old sluice, I noticed the bottom of my gold pan gradually turning yellow. I could not believe my eyes, for the more I worked the pan, the more gold appeared. A whole ounce in one pan! There I was, out in the middle of nowhere, jumping around doing a little miners jig and surely frightening all local game back into the wilds from which they may have been peering. My addictive personality took over completely and before I realized what was happening, I had requested some time off and returned to the dredge. I made camp and threw myself wholeheartedly into searching out more of this elusive metal. Sadly, there were no more pans full of gold dust, but I did recover a total of five ounces throughout the summer. I realized I would have to be on my guard against this insane obsession that had driven so many miners over the brink of despair.

An old friend, Ken, came up to pay us a visit. He wanted to see what was keeping so many of us out of civilization for months at a time. Chuck asked me to give him a tour of the area, including other mines. We spent a few days learning how others processed gold and I came to realize there are as many different techniques as there are miners.

One evening, back in our camp, Ken called for me to come over to the other side of the bunkhouse.

"Ron, have a look at that," he whispered.

Following the direction of his pointed finger, I exclaimed, "Wow, that's awesome!"

On the other side of a narrow strip of trees were ten wolves frolicking, completely oblivious to our existence. They were running about the meadow nipping and pouncing on one another with playful glee. What a delight it was to witness these huge beasts in their natural habitat, untamed and unmolested. These animals were doing as they had for ions, and were not about to let our presence impede their basic instincts. This was the first time I had seen a whole pack of wolves in the wild, previously only viewing one or two at a time. The only photo taken was the one implanted in the minds of Ken and myself, but surely, one neither of us would soon forget.

Another close encounter with the best that nature had to offer were a pair of lynx who watched me intently while I was gold panning. Their tufted ears and piercing eyes drew my attention away from the pursuit of gold for a considerable time. Their curiosity was amazing, as human encroachment had not affected them as of yet, nor would it likely in the near future in this beautifully wild and immense land.

On another occasion, while travelling to town, I rounded a bend in the trail and met a lone, large caribou running directly toward me. He stopped abruptly, turned about and trotted directly away from me. He headed straight down the trail, his gangly legs seeming to go every which way. I marvelled at the way this animal was adapted to this northern country with his very wide hooves, thick coat of hair and the adornment of horns. To say this was a "he" is really only speculation, as both females and males of this species have horns. I did not have the time to check out the rest of the anatomy.

With such a short growing season, flowers popped up with an intense blast of color for approximately a week or so, and then disappeared as quickly as they came. Fireweed, purple flowers, yellow blooms and many forms of plant life abounded in this short time frame. Not being a horticulturist, all I could really do was just enjoy their beauty, be it a weed or flower.

Relics from the past were also plentiful. I found a mammoth tusk, which, once freed from its icy domicile, had immediately started to decay. The scent emitted was one like none other I had ever encountered. It was humbling to hold something so ancient, forcing me to reflect on how miniscule our time on earth really is.

More recent artifacts unearthed included shovels, picks, charred wood and other mining items. The miners of old would pick and shovel their way in the riverbed during the winter months, burning timbers to melt the frost. They worked all winter, hoisting the gold bearing gravel from the bottom of these holes and then carting it to the shoreline. Come spring, they would begin processing it on shore while the water poured into the icy holes they had dug in the middle of the river. The following season they would have to start anew, as the solid cake of ice prevented them re-entering their previous digs. While I sat in the heated cab of my front-end loader feeding the screener, I tried to fathom the hardships mankind had endured in the quest for gold.

The season wore down and we got our first snowfall near the beginning of September. We had to cease our operation due to ice forming on the matting used to capture the gold. Now we commenced repairing the machinery, which we had worked to the extreme, due to the short window of summer.

One evening I arrived in camp to discover that three young Austrian adventurers had ambled out of the forest. They had canoed down the Stewart River to where it entered the Yukon River and then had struck off into the bush following an old, overgrown trail. Their mission was to find the site of Jack London's cabin. The cabin had long since been removed, half now existing in Dawson City, the other half in San Francisco. However, the site that it had occupied lay about three kilometres north of our camp, up Little Henderson Creek.

One of the young men had experienced more wild and cold than he could endure and had lost his sense of reason. He had struck out for Dawson on foot in the snow. He did not comprehend what he was undertaking or how unforgiving this uninhabited land could be. The first camp he would encounter if successful was fifty kilometres from ours. I set out in the dark, tracing his tracks in the snow and was shocked to see that he was not sticking to the trail, but rather taking short cuts cutting across frozen swamps. My worry now turned to urgency as I searched for his tracks at each point where he should have returned to the trail. He was truly on a suicide mission (even if he did not realize it). My goal became obvious; I had to rescue him from himself. I reached a spot where his footprints did not return to the road and deep sense of foreboding overtook me.

I stepped out of the truck and shone my flashlight into the dark forest. Peering into the direction he should be coming from, I perceived some movement. Sure enough, there he came, trudging through the thickness of the night. He had a heavy pack on his back, was hunched over and plodded along very slowly. I called out, but he did not respond. I waited as he slowly made his way to my position.

Relieved, yet equally annoyed, I demanded, "What are you doing?"

"I no speak English," he replied.

Not deterred, I went on, "You can't survive out here. It's about a hundred and sixty kilometres to Dawson City. The closest miner is still about forty kilometres from here."

"I go to Dawson," was all he said.

"No, you have to return with me to the camp and your friends. You can't go further."

"I go to Dawson."

Although obviously tired, he was also suffering from a minor mental breakdown, the kind that occurs when people surpass their perceived level of endurance. I had seen this before more than once. I knew I had to divert this fellow from his suicide mission in order for him to regain his sanity. I finally relented and told him I would get him out to the first mine, where perhaps someone was going into town or where we could contact the R.C.M.P. Somehow, I managed to get him to understand some of this, although I am sure all he cared about was that we were going forward, not back.

We arrived late at the neighbouring mine and I explained the situation to the boss there. He informed me that he was heading to town in the morning, and would gladly take this fellow there. I managed to convey this to the Austrian and he nodded his head in agreement. The heat inside the cab of the truck had assailed his tired and cold body, rendering him less resistant. Fatigue was overtaking him. He quietly accompanied the friendly neighbour to the warm confines of their bunkhouse.

As Robert Service the poet noted, strange things do happen in the 'Land of the Midnight Sun'. Not long after this incident, I received a message that my father was to undergo heart surgery. I bid farewell to the crew, to the Yukon and headed south.

Chapter 9

THE TIMING OF my arrival in Edmonton could not have been more precise. My father was preparing to go in for a new heart valve the following day and I joined the family on a tour of the intensive care unit to prepare us for what lay ahead. This all turned out to be of no avail, for when I visited my father after his operation, I agonized watching him attempting to breath. There were tubes coming out of every orifice of his body.

The following day I returned to the intensive care unit and they told me Dad was no longer there. He was back in his ward! When I entered the room, I was astounded to see the man who was in such suffering the previous day, now sitting in a chair beside his bed. He was a smiling marvel of twentieth century medicine.

While he was recovering with the tender care of his sister, Mother and I made a trip to Mesa, Arizona, liquidating everything they owned there. We packed the car as full as we could with personal effects and left all else behind, including many tools, much to the chagrin of my father. On the way home we stopped in Las Vegas to help pay for the trip (which in fact my mother did), while I just added further to my debt load. Near Flagstaff, a hailstorm thoroughly dented the car, and gave my father one more thing to admonish us for. Perhaps this is why he recovered so rapidly, in case the need for his supervision was required for any future ventures.

Now it was time to get back to work and start building capital to head back to South America. I settled into an apartment in Calgary, got back to my program in earnest and started doing what was right for Ron. My next job took me once more into the north, and the most stressful situation I have ever encountered in the course of my entire working career. Due to the confidential nature of that employment, I am at liberty only to describe the environment in which I now found myself immersed.

I had previously worked in Yellowknife, N.W.T. twice before and had grown fond of this vibrant, eccentric city. I now found a community divided due to the violent strike at the local mine. Nine men had been murdered, several bombing incidents had taken place and a violent riotous takeover of the mine sight had occurred. "Scabs" and families versus "strikers" and families, with outsiders unavoidably taking sides created a seemingly irreparable situation. Some children, who had grown up as friends, were now fighting in the schoolyard supporting their parent's views.

After working only a couple of months in this environment, I took a week off and went to Mazatlan, Mexico for a little stress relief. I returned to more strife, and found the short break had done little to accomplish what I had hoped. Shortly thereafter, I left the northern capital. When the plane lifted me out of the turmoil below, a loud sigh of relief escaped from my lips. At the time, I felt the internal wounds of the city would be impossible to heal, but a new influx of people came in on the new diamond discoveries at a very opportune time, helping diffuse the negative local milieu.

Back in the big city, I began job-hunting again, something at which I was becoming quite proficient. An ad in the local newspaper caught my eye…and curiosity.

"Wanted: 1 administrator for an oil firm working in Venezuela."

Could it be? My life seemed like a series of ironies, and this looked like another one was about to be added to the list.

I acquired the address and made my way into the maze of sky-scraper businesses known as downtown Calgary. I entered the large edifice that held the address I was seeking and made my way up the elevator to the designated floor. Arriving at the door with the address number on it, I was surprised to see that there was no company nameplate. I opened the door and walked in, taking a quick glance around to see if there was any indication naming this company. There was none apparent, so I approached the receptionist,

"Hi. Could you please tell me what the name of this company is?"

"Sure," she said, "It's Destiny Drilling."

"Would Adrian happen to be here?"

"Can I tell him who is calling?" she asked.

"You sure can," I replied. "Tell him Ron is here to see him."

When Adrian came up the hall and seen me, he stopped short. After an awkward pause on his part, I said,

"I think you and I have something to talk about."

He invited me into his office and apologized profusely for the fiasco that had transpired on my last trip south. This time, I was neither hasty nor about to accept any verbal promises. After some negotiation, we drew up an agreement and I was destined for Venezuela again. This time Destiny paid for my plane ticket. More importantly, I now had a contract in my hand.

Returning home to my little apartment, I had time to sit and reflect on all that had transpired since my first encounter with Adrian. The 'chance' meeting was no coincidence (a word that no longer fits my vocabulary). I was originally hired at an office located eight-hundred kilometres away from this location. It seemed that the comedy of errors on the first endeavour had allowed me to prepare more fully for what now lay ahead. Learning Spanish was one key element. Even Adrian had been impressed on how well I had progressed with this new language.

Another thing that had become apparent, from my previous trip south, was that I had strayed from my positive way of living. Frequenting bars and lounges in the course of my 'Spanish lessons', had been a form of 'Russian Roulette.' This time I would need to make a concerted effort to practice living the twelve-step program that had protected me thus far. God was allowing me this fantastic opportunity and providing me the tools to work with. Now it was up to me to use them. Moreover, it would be imperative to recognize when He was nudging me. I had come to believe strongly that, not only did my Higher Power have a great deal of patience with me, but also a good deal of grace.

My first task was to get some equipment loaded on a truck headed for Houston. There it would be loaded on a ship destined for Venezuela. My truck was included with this shipment as the use of it had been included in the contract. We had the two pieces of equipment loaded on the semi-trailer and were in the process of loading my pick-up when I got a phone call. I was informed that my vehicle could not be brought into the country! It was a used unit and the duty would be more than a new vehicle would cost. Now I had a dilemma. What was I to do with my truck with things happening so fast? Then along came another positive nudge from my Higher Power. One of the fellows who had sold us the equipment offered to buy my truck for the asking price. With cash in hand, I was quickly relieved of another responsibility.

Once the equipment arrived in Venezuela, I was to fly there, learn how to cut jungle with it, and then train the locals on how to use it. One machine was a Ford tractor with a double blade bush cutting apparatus mounted on the front lift assembly. The other was a bobcat with a similar attachment, but with only one blade. Once I had proven the equipment was viable, and had trained operators, I would assume the administrative duties.

While the equipment was in transit, I liquidated the newly acquired effects of my little apartment, spent a lot of time with my friends in the fellowship, as well as some quality time with family. Finally, the day arrived and I was once more boarding a plane for the land of adventure, this time not quite so naive, a little better prepared, and as enthusiastic as ever.

END PART I

PART II

Chapter 10

MY FIRST ATTEMPT to live in Venezuela had been enlightening and had laid the groundwork for what lay ahead. The novelty of my freedom to pursue varied female companionships had lost its lustre and getting down to business became my number one priority. Entering Venezuela was not nearly as intimidating this time as I now had a better idea of how the system worked. Still, none of the waving placards displayed by the multitudes of people at the airport had my name on it; some things had not changed. Since no one was there to meet me, I headed for familiar territory, the Las Americas Hotel. At least this time, Fred, the country manager, answered the phone and acknowledged my existence.

I was introduced to Ciro (a Venezuelan who spoke perfect English), who was to assist us getting the equipment through customs and out to the job-sites. Together we tackled the bureaucracy and I got a taste of what doing business here consisted of. Paperwork did not move without the 'greasing of palms'. At first this seemed rather simple, but as I became more versed in the art of getting things done, I learned that there was a system to paying people off. The amount, to whom, when and where all had to be factored in to be effective.

We also discovered that a box of tools placed in one of the machines back in Canada was missing. This had not been a particularly bright idea, as their portability and value made them a tempting target for light fingers.

"How are we going to get these people to turn over those tools?" I asked Carlos.

"No problem," was his response, one I soon learned to dread hearing.

That mechanic never did recover his tools, nor was there any compensation.

One day, during this initiation process, I left my computer in my hotel room. When I returned, the hotel staff had moved my gear and placed it in another room. All seemed in order, but when I attempted to turn on the computer, the monitor was blank. It appeared the maid had set down the briefcase containing the computer a little bit too roughly. Now I really faced a dilemma. One of the largest buildings in Caracas is the IBM building, so that is where I proceeded. It turned out to be a head office and not a place to take a brand new computer that had given up the ghost. However, they did direct me to a little repair shop in one of the back streets. Taking a cab made finding the place easy. The technician was knowledgeable and friendly, but it was with considerable reservation that I left him with my sole expensive possession.

I was astonished when I returned the following day and he handed me a brand new computer, complete with a Spanish keyboard.

"Su computadora necesita ser reparada y esto significará mandando su computadora," the tech explained.

The tech had just informed me the monitor in my computer was finished, and he would need to send it out for repair. Thus, he gave me a new computer, set it up and transferred all my files to it, at no cost.

"Yo tengo mucho agradecer," I said, thanking him.

My 'Spanish lessons' were paying off, and was impressed that I comprehended this whole transaction. Moreover, I was quite pleased with how easily everything had unfolded, especially when

I reflected on the previous day at customs. This was truly a country of contrasts.

Finally, the equipment was loaded on a truck and sent off to Sta. Maria de Ipire, located in the middle of the state of Guarico. Into the ranching country of central Venezuela I went. The company had rented a house, and this served both as residence and office for the five of us North Americans. The party chief was French-Canadian and the rest of the crew were Americans.

"You missed all the excitement," Pascal, the party chief, informed me.

"Yes, if you had arrived yesterday you wouldn't have gotten in here," said Drew, the mechanic.

"Why is that?" my curiosity begged to know.

"The workers got all upset over some crazy thing and decided to go on strike. They set a bunch of tires on fire in our driveway. We've been penned in here for a couple of days. Today is the first time we've been able to drive out of the yard," Pascal replied.

"What am I getting myself into?" I asked, laughing.

With that interchange, I was welcomed into the crew and made myself at home.

The next day I proceeded to cut jungle with the Ford brush cutter, with a trail of ten men walking behind with machetes and chainsaws. They equated this machine to job losses and were having no part of that. Time was of the essence, so we put up with the nonsense. The rainy season would soon be upon us, ending oil exploration activities in this area. In dried up riverbeds lay dead caiman, in what had been the last pools of water. Cattle were ribcage Brahmas, looking like they would never fatten up. The grass was so dry that I started a fire accidentally when the blades on my machine scratched a rock. All of this made it hard for me to fathom what the rainy season would be like.

One day, while cutting down lianas and working my way through the jungle forming a new seismic line, I looked behind to find the crew had disappeared. Not knowing what happened, I got out of the machine and started to walk back down the line. Suddenly several bees began buzzing around my face, soon joined by more. Due to their aggressive behaviour, I quickly realized these were African bees. I had heard they were in the area, but hadn't paid much attention to that information at the time. Now I was paying a lot of attention, and so were they. I hunched over, covered my ears with my hands, my eyes with my elbows and then ran like a madman. They swarmed me, but when I got about sixty feet from where they first attacked, they retreated. Due to my long sleeved shirt, the rapid exit and no doubt a little divine intervention, I did not receive one sting. I then found out that the crew had taken one fellow to the hospital who was stung severely. In fact, most of the crew was stung at least a couple of times.

These bees were a constant hazard, so we purchased full protection gear and had no problem getting the crew to use it. What made these particular bees such a menace was their aggressive behaviour and relentless attacks when defending their territory. Despite this inconvenience, I found them quite fascinating. When they came into an area, they arrived as a large grey mass humming through the clear blue skies. Once they settled into an area, they broke off into clusters forming hives inside rotten tree trunks.

Each time we discovered them on our seismic line, the bee suit was donned, the tree was cut down and the hive was burned. Noise really upset these little black-striped furies. On one occasion, I had to shut off my machine and wait until these agitated insects settled down. I was eye level with their home and had a first hand look into the life and times of the African Bee. However, with doors and windows closed up tight, and no air conditioner running, I did not remain long marvelling at their antics.

Using the machines to cut seismic line lasted a total of three weeks, at which time the union managed to curtail their use under the auspices of environmental control. The crew then resumed cutting the line by hand, as originally intended. I moved into the office and undertook the administration duties. Of all the gringos on our crew, I seemed to be the least intimidated by speaking Spanish and so ended up relegated to the task of dealing with the union boss.

Their demands at times were ludicrous. One morning, I awoke and headed outdoors to our bathroom building, and the union boss cut me off.

"Jefe," he demanded, "nos quieremos mas hielo."

My bladder had no time for interruption. We exchanged some harsh words that nearly erupted into a fistfight. I pushed past him, took care of nature and then returned to find out what their dire needs were. It turned out they wanted two, not just one, bags of ice in each water jug. For this, they were prepared to go on strike. Had they been working for any local company, they would have been fortunate to get luke-warm water.

The Spanish dialect spoke in this area was very fast, crude and difficult to understand. Even the people in Caracas had a hard time understanding people from this province. The 'vaqueros' had their own form of swearing and slang. They were a fun loving bunch, once away from leadership of the union, and were the source of many a good laugh. Life was lived for the moment and 'mañana' was irrelevant. Once they gave me some cowboy chewing tobacco that had me puking over the tailgate. Yes, they did have a sense of humour. These men would stop their swearing and make the holy cross every time they passed the shrine to Sta. Maria, which was by the roadside. This amazed me as the truck box was enclosed and they could not see when they were approaching the sacred spot, but somehow intuitively knew when it was near.

Once that project was completed, we took the employees that were not union, our forty per cent of the labour force, and moved west to El Dividivi. There, a new crew was hired, the sixty per cent union requirement. This crew would end up being the best one we were to have in the country, and for that reason, this six-month project would prove to be the most profitable undertaken in the two years I was with Destiny.

The move proved more adventurous than anticipated. According to the map, there appeared to be a shortcut that would cut many miles off the journey. Always being one to take a shorter route if possible, I embarked on this journey alone, pulling a trailer behind a Toyota pickup. On the trailer were two drills mounted sideways, which caused me to be over width on both sides of the trailer. The first part of the journey went relatively smooth; I even handled the Guardia at the alcabalas without any problems. Of course, most of these check stops cost me a little, but I was prepared for that. I had different denominations of Bolivars in my pocket. If an older guard came out, I knew it was going to cost me, but with a younger one, I could usually get through for next to nothing. They could always find something wrong with the documentation, whether it was the truck, trailer, cargo or me!

Once I started to climb up over the Sierra Nevada, life got very interesting. My goal: get over the mountains during daylight hours. At first, the scenery was dazzling and the thrill of this unique experience permeated my soul. This was what I had come to South America for! As I progressed upward, the green jungle unravelled its marvellous beauty, seeming to call my heart into its mysterious depths. On the steep hillsides there were farmers working their coffee fields. Just walking on these steep inclines must be a task, let alone climbing, planting and working with these fastidious plants. At times, I even observed a donkey traversing these slopes with his master.

The road gradually became steeper, narrower and the corners sharper. My enchantment was slowly turning to concern as the day was getting late and my progress was slow. I now was on a road that not even the mini buses were using. On some corners, I had to back up and jackknife my rig to make it around the bend. In one such place, a waterfall cascaded onto the road, creating a natural car wash. Some portions had vertical cliffs on both sides of the road, straight up, and straight down. However, my nervousness did not really start to crest until I entered a small village up in the mountains. The streets were so steep that I had to put the truck in four-wheel drive while on dry concrete!

However, the reason for my sudden apprehension was what I derived from my surroundings. All of the dwellings implied wealth. Gone were the simple homes of the common people. Everyone seemed to be driving new vehicles and prosperity was visible every-where. This was not a resort town, so my mind immediately began to assume the worst; it appeared that I might have just stumbled into cocaine country. Coca plants were abundant, giving substance to my worries. Moreover, the majority of men I observed seemed rough looking, a very different class of people than I had seen so far in my southern journeys. My mind was now working overtime as I observed every passing vehicle and its inhabitants with suspicion. Fear started to envelope me as the shadow of night cloaked the countryside.

The road didn't allow for hasty passage and soon I found myself winding through this mountain corridor in the pitch black of night. Although I did not encounter many vehicles, there were locals walking on the side of the road. I had to be careful I didn't knock a peasant over the side of the mountain with my overly wide load. This was a very real possibility. With my headlights shining into their eyes that were accustomed to darkness, these souls could not see my overhanging load. I finally made it down the other side of the mountain, hopeful that I never hit anyone – the uncertainty of that haunts my mind to this day.

Entering a more traditional town than the previous ones, I now found myself trying to negotiate my wide load down a very narrow main street. On my right side, the hitches of the drills were whisping past parked vehicles. On my left, the drills were flirting with the air conditioners protruding from the windows of the buildings. The townspeople, seeing my predicament, came to the rescue and guided me the length of the street, directing me left, right and straight ahead. Being super friendly people, they then pointed me in the direction of a hotel at the bottom of the hill that had parking for a large rig such as mine. With a sigh of relief, I arrived at my safe haven around ten pm. I was exhausted, but safe. I said a very special prayer of thanks that evening before retiring, ever grateful that God's servant, my Guide, had led me safely down the mountain.

The next day I completed my journey to El Dividivi without incident. After recounting my ordeal in the mountains, no one else attempted that route. My first solo voyage had been traumatic, but I had survived and gained some confidence in the process. I had proven to myself that I could get around independently, and to me, that was very important. Of course, I recognized I had not been completely alone.

Chapter 11

"So, how long did they hold you hostage?" I asked Clint. "The rebels moved me all over the jungle for about five weeks," he drawled.

I was sitting with our new mechanic at the back of our house, amongst the drilling equipment. He had just been ransomed out of the hands of the Columbian Rebels and now he had to pay back all those good people who were so kind to come up with the money. I now had a chance to pick his brain about all that had transpired and could do so uninterrupted. Clint was originally from the same area of Northern Alberta as me. Twenty years previous, he had moved to this southern country and set up a very small fishing camp in Los Llanos. It wasn't a big money maker, but it fed him and his Venezuelan family amply.

"How did they get you when your camp was so far inland from the Columbian border?"

"I have a local pilot I use to save these softies from having to travel hours over rough road into the interior. He landed his Cessna on our little grass airstrip to pick up five very successful fishermen who were anxious to get home to brag about their catch." Clint leaned back casually, his easy soft-spoken demeanour not belying the ordeal he had just experienced.

"When the pilot shut off the engine," he went on, "we started walking toward the plane. Suddenly, a bunch of rebels sprung out of the high grass and surrounded us. They were waving their guns and yelling. Things got real chaotic. They were so crazed it was hard to understand what they were saying or what was happening. They forced everyone back, then grabbed me and one of my clients and pushed us into the plane. Four of the radicals got in with us and told the pilot to take off. It happened that fast. Still hard to believe."

"Wow, you must have been some scared!" I exclaimed.

"Yes, sure glad they didn't shoot anyone. Those four fishermen they left behind had the scare of their lives."

Clint continued, "Everything happened so fast. It wasn't until we set out towards Columbia that things started to register. But there was no talking to them. They seemed to be hopped up on something – totally irrational. So, we just kept our mouths shut. I am sure glad that my client, Ed, was the kind of fellow he was. He didn't get aggressive with these guys or shoot his mouth off. That could've made things real bad."

Having only known Clint a short while, I had already pegged him as a very practical person, but he was also extremely laid back. He had lived in this country for a long time and had adapted a slow manner of speech and living, which showed as he related this harrowing experience.

"So, where did they take you?"

"We landed on a little strip in the jungle, must have been two hours flying from my place, so it was a fair ways into Columbia. When we got there, what a reception! There was a whole crew there, all excited as hell, waving their guns all over, shooting off a few shots in the air all wild-like. I overheard them talking about the millions they were going to get for us. That is when my hopes started to sink. These idiots knew nothing about money, and they sure as hell weren't going to get that kind of money for me. Nobody I knew had that kind of doe."

Then Clint shared how he managed to get things a bit under control in a very unorthodox manner.

"When things finally settled down, I got the ring leader away from the others, and asked him if he had a bullet in that gun of his. You can imagine the look on his face. I told him if he did, would he kindly put it right here." Clint placed a finger in the centre of his forehead.

"I told him I didn't feel like being dragged around the jungle for months knowing damn well they were never going to get what they were asking. So if they weren't going to be reasonable, just end it now. Well, did that ever get his attention. Fortunately, as you can see, he didn't take me up on my offer. But after that they did get more sensible and sat about discussing what would be a reasonable demand. Eventually they came up with a price and then the waiting game began."

"That must have been some difficult, sitting there and not knowing what was going to happen next. How did you handle it?" I asked.

"They actually treated us pretty good, and fed us the same as themselves. The only thing they wouldn't let us near or have was their women," Clint chuckled. "They did drag us around the jungle quite a bit, changing locations every time a plane flew over or some other incident made them edgy. I have to give it to ole Ed; he turned out to be a real trooper, certainly not a softy like so many of his compatriots. At least I understood the language. He had the added burden of not understanding what was going on every time there was some change happening."

A rooster crowed, causing Clint and I to burst into laughter; these Venezuelan cocks didn't have any sense of time. Their rude interruptions could come at any time of day. Ignoring the rooster's call for recognition, Clint was quickly able to resume where he had left off. He continued to share his experience with me, reliving his ordeal

"Well, after about five weeks, my associate in the States flew to Bogota with a suitcase full of money. He rented a car, got a crude map and drove into the jungle to an area they had somehow agreed upon. This was quite a frightening experience for him. Somehow he found us, the money exchanged hands and they turned us loose.

"Wow, that must have been a relief," I said.

"Well, first of all, we didn't know what was going on; we thought this was just another move. I was pretty shocked when we were brought to a roadside and there stood my partner. He looked scared shitless. Things happened fast and once we were in his car and moving, then we all breathed a big sigh of relief. We had a long way to go through rebel country, so we didn't really relax until we were safely back in the city. There we finally unwound. A steak was certainly in order," he said, laughing.

"Once in Bogota we had a big hassle getting visas out of the country as I had no passport or anything. After we got a hold of the Canadian Embassy, things levelled out. I flew back here to Venezuela with the pilot, while my associate and Ed went north."

"That's quite a story. Did you get questioned by the police or anyone once it was over?"

"That was the weird part." Here Clint got pensive. "The DEA contacted me and said they wanted to interview me and find out where all these rebel camps were. I never heard from them again. Then a writer from some magazine contacted me and asked if he could write my story. I said sure, but that was the only time I heard from him."

"So, here you are twisting wrenches instead of guiding fishermen. Are you going to resume your guide business?"

"I have to make a lot of money to pay back all those who chipped in to get me out of there. Think I am going to be here awhile," Clint despaired.

Not long after my conversation with Clint, I had an unnerving incident of my own. It happened when I went to the closest city, Valera. I was driving slowly in the left-hand lane looking for a street that would allow me to turn left. A car drove up behind me honking his horn. Annoyed, I hit my brakes. Road rage kicked in and I slowed down even more. The little, red sports car pulled out and passed me on the right, then cut back in front of me, coming to a complete stop. I jammed on my brakes and quickly realized the situation was turning serious. A burly man jumped out of the car and came straight to my vehicle. I grabbed the door handle, prepared to swing the door into his legs if things got out of hand. He was red in the face and stormed up beside my vehicle shouting a lot of stuff I didn't understand. I said the first thing that came to my head.

"Fuck off!"

I knew that was something he would understand. I had learned that the use of this explicative down here had added impact in that the people took it as a complete assault on their person. He went ballistic. His speech became garbled. Finally, he did something I did understand. He reached into his pocket, pulled out his wallet and showed me his identification. He was the Chief of Police! Now I wasn't such a smart ass. He demanded my passport, my driver's license, my cedula, my registration and anything else he could think of. I didn't have a passport, so I gave him my transient cedula (a form of Venezuelan ID) along with my other documents. He then told me to go to the police station.

"Yo lo seguiré." I told him I would follow him.

"No, vaya al estacion directamente," he blasted at me, and walked to his car.

Since he had all my documentation, I wasn't about to let him out of my sight. I followed him, assuming he would be going to the police station. I was mistaken. He headed out of town into the mountainous countryside. And he wasn't alone. There was another man in the car with him. Insanity had obviously overtaken me, as I pursued them. I figured I was being set up for a beating, but now, swept up in the motion of events, there seemed to be no turning back. They drove, up a twisty, windy road. Finally slowing down, they signalled to turn left off the highway. This was the moment of truth and my gut turned. Then, to my surprise, they turned into a Country Club, with me right on their tail. This apparently was too much for them, so the big fellow got out his car, came back and threw all my papers at me. Once again I was told to go directly to the station.

"Si, señor," I said, and drove off. Of course, I got out of town as fast as I could and used a different vehicle on future trips to Valera. I found out later why the chief had been so upset. The local law requires that you drive in the right lane, let all traffic pass, and then cut all the way across the left lane to make your turn. The left lane is for the people in a hurry. A crazy system, but it was theirs. They certainly weren't going to change it on my account.

Another incident in Valera revealed how inappropriately I was handling my stress level. Some money transferred down from Canada a couple of weeks previously still had not appeared in our account. I knew that someone at the bank was holding this large sum of money in their personal bank account and making fast interest from it. I went berserk, creating a big scene in the bank. I confronted the bank manager, loudly and aggressively, in front of both his clients and staff. After threatening him with police intervention, I stormed out of the bank. I sheepishly returned several weeks later and was surprised at the welcome I received. They treated me with total respect, and, ironically, money transfers began to get through in an acceptable amount of time. Slowly I was learning local customs and ways.

On one of these excursions to the city of Valera, I was accompanied by a young fellow fresh from Canada. This was his first time out of his native land, and he was constantly proclaiming about the way we should help these people. As we drove by yet another little farm with people living in houses made of clay, an old pickup parked in the driveway and a cow in the field, again he piped up,

"We have to help these people. Look how they live."

"Look at their faces," I told him.

"What do you mean?"

"These people aren't living in poverty. On the contrary. The smiles on their faces show they have the type of contentment we can only dream of. That farmer owns his house, his land, his old truck and his cow. In the land we come from, very few people can say that. The banks own it all, and we work for the banks."

I pointed out to him that we were the ones zooming along at one-hundred and twenty kilometres per hour, trying to get to the bank on time. They sat smiling, watching us crazy gringos caught in our time machine. To them, time is unimportant. What they did not accomplish today, they can do mañana. Really, who is living in poverty? If our debts were called in tomorrow, I'm sure we would be far worse off than that farmer who hasn't bought into the concept that more is better.

That said, I realized that the culture I came from was too in-grained, and no doubt it would be very difficult, if not impossible, for me to assimilate these people's laissez-faire manner of living.

I soon learned that to deal with these everyday stresses, I had to change my present pattern of handling them. I did not have any meetings available, as that resource was non-existent in this area. Walking has always been a good method for me to unwind, yet whenever I did that in the local communities, I was constantly bombarded with requests for employment from the locals. Thus began my retreats from the computer, unions and any other sources of stress. My first trip was to Merida, high in the Andes. There I rented a motorbike and roared through the enchanting valleys. I found a park, very similar to Jasper in Alberta, with pine trees and log shelters. I laid down on the grass beside a stream and fell asleep for two hours. What an experience! It was apparent that this was a much-needed break. Returning to the turmoil of daily living after a week of repose, my refortified self could once again handle the challenges thrust at me. And there were to be many more challenges ahead!

Chapter 12

CORRUPTION AND VENEZUELA; two words I found seemingly synonymous. It was 1992 and President Perez's government and people knew no bounds when it came to corruption. The various manifestations of this permeated Venezuelan society completely and it was utterly rife within the work place. At times, this corruption could work to one's advantage, but for the most part, it was truly an adversity to overcome.

As a sub-contractor, our men were paid by the contractor, and this amount deducted from our earnings. The labour code of the country is, in itself, very intricate, and compounded with the union code, the whole process was almost undecipherable. The contractor used an elaborate computer program to calculate wages but they would not give us access to it.

Therefore, taking the Union's Blue Book and the Government's Red Book (the two labour law guidelines), I set out to double check the amount we should be billed for wages. This involved many agonizing hours at the computer creating a spreadsheet that would reveal the truth. After several weeks, I accomplished my mission, and from there it took no time to do the necessary calculations. I was astounded at the findings. So was the contractor. When I walked in and accused them of gouging us for more than $60,000 in less than three months, they could not deny the facts. They hastily paid back the money.

Crossing private land was yet another ordeal. The local farmers had been paid for land usage, but spotted an opportunity to line their pockets even more with all these foreigners about. Several of them decided that they would not let us cut and mend the barbed-wire fences, which was the normal practice. They demanded we pay an amount for each fence cut, or use the gate, which was impractical most of the time due to distance and terrain.

We decided that if we couldn't go through, then we would go up and over. Some aluminium ramps were manufactured in Canada, which then allowed us to go pigsty fashion over the fences with our quad motor bikes pulling the small drills. The farmers were shocked by our ingenuity, and relented. We resumed cutting the fences and our expensive ramps were retired to the back yard to gather dust.

Moving about required us passing a certain check stop on a regular basis. This always cost us money, or something of value. To alleviate that problem we purchased a desk for the Guardia, as well as some other big-ticket items. From then on, we passed through hassle free. Tires bought for the local police car, tickets purchased for every community project and other forms of adding our bit to the local economy were essential. These actions aided us in having a positive relationship with the military, law and citizens.

Normally quite passive people, these local Venezuelans could also become quite volatile. This became especially apparent one day as I returned from the field driving our Toyota pickup. On the Pan-American Highway, just as I entered El Dividive, traffic had come to a complete stop. I could not see what the problem was, so I decided to pull out and pass the line up since my exit into town was just a short distance away.

Suddenly I saw numerous large rocks scattered all over the road. My first thought was that a truck had lost its load. Then a man with a bandana over his face ran in front of me, forcing me to stop. I quickly surveyed the scene and it finally dawned on me what was going on. I was in the middle of a riot. On my right was a bunch of men wearing bandanas over their faces, throwing large rocks across the highway at the police, who were protecting themselves with shields. Some of these rocks were flung right over my truck. Although I now found myself in a quite a predicament, I couldn't help but chuckle, for I recognized one of these fellows as a local, despite his bandana. It wasn't that hard to do. He was the only midget in town. I quickly realized the others were townsfolk as well, so I motioned for one of them to come over to my truck. As he approached the truck, I said,

"Yo vivo aquí, tu me conoces. Por favor permítame pasar."

Having told him I lived there, he recognized me, and motioned me to go down through the ditch, past the crowd and into town.

"What the heck is going on down at the highway," I asked the cook when I got back to the house.

"Los gentes no tienen agua por dos semanas," Rose shared with me. The people had been without running water for two weeks due to corrupt officials taking money designated for the water supply and using it for their own purposes. As Rose filled me in on the local problem, my eyes started to burn. The police had taken action, teargassed the mob and we were receiving the residual. Sure enough, that ended the battle, but the people had won; they had water the next day. The lack of water had not affected us since we had installed a water tank as soon as we moved into our house. Foresight saved us this added aggravation.

On another occasion, further on down the road, I once again had to drive into the ditch, this time against the will of the masses. Striking teachers had placed burning tires all over the highway. I blasted by these people, receiving heat not only from the fire, but from the hostile strikers as well. Hot Latin tempers were flying!

One day I received a call from Fred in Caracas.

"Ron, we have been accused of 'short-holing'. What's going on over there?"

Short-holing was a term used to describe when the dynamite is not placed all the way down the drill hole; it was a serious charge. This was going to result in false seismic recordings. This meant that the complete seismic line would need to be re-drilled. The contractor claimed to have photos of our 'taquedor' loading several holes in this fashion. This could end our working in the oil industry any-where in the country as our company would then be black listed.

"I'll have some of the boys find out what's going on," I replied.

Fortunately, by now, we had some loyal employees and they set out to find out what was really happening. What we uncovered was deviousness and corruption beyond belief.

The contractor's surveyors had staked out the line for us to cut, drill and load. We then proceeded to drill holes and load them with dynamite. After we had covered about two miles, someone realized that the line was not on the proper coordinates. This was going to be a major loss of money and probably somebody's high paying job. A scheme was created to divert the attention onto us; they were at-tempting to cover up their mistake. One of our own employees was paid a good sum of money to deliberately tamp the dynamite part way down the hole, while another fellow stood in the bushes and took pictures.

Of course, the contractor's main office in Caracas was unaware of the major error in calculations, so once we passed on that infor-mation, the rest all fell into place and we were exonerated. There were constant attempts by the local bosses to get rid of us, as they wanted to make this job last a long time. In other words, we were too productive. But we did successfully complete that project, and made money doing so.

"Well Brent, after that fiasco I need a break," I said to the project manager.

"Where to, Canada?"

"No, on the contrary, south, into the jungle, where maybe things are a little more civilized," I replied, laughing.

"Go for it," Brent responded. I bolted for the door before another crisis arose that would change his decision.

Flying six hours from Caracas to Rio de Janeiro, down across the equator, gave me an opportunity to see just how immense the Amazon forest really is. Once in Rio, I boarded a plane to Manaus and flew an additional four hours over this blanket of green.

Expecting to see the jungle ablaze, I was quite surprised to see the contrary. Looking down I could see where the locals had attempted to clear some small areas by fire, but these had quickly grown over. It seemed impossible to me that any significant amount of the jungle would burn with so much water around. I was arriving in the flood season, so actual land became sparse as the mighty river and its tributaries spread their murky water around the trees and over smaller vegetation. During my twenty hour flight over the Amazon Rainforest, I saw a total of three small fires, none of them burning with the magnitude of a small forest fire in Canada.

When I landed in Manaus, I was inundated with humidity and tour promoters. As Portuguese was the central language, I brushed off these speculators like the sweat off my brow, until I found one who spoke not only Spanish, but English as well.

"Hi, my name is Ron," I said introducing myself.

"Mine is Juan," responded the tour promoter.

"What I'm looking for is something a little different than what you're used to Juan. Since you speak English and Spanish, I think we might be able to work something out. I'm going to tell you what I'm looking for, and you tell me if you can find it for me, ok?"

"What is it you are looking for, Señor Ron?"

"I want to rent a boat with a Captain, cook and maybe you as a guide. I want to go up river and away from tourists. I don't want anyone else on the boat, and I want a captain willing to go where I want. I don't want to go to all the normal tourist spots. Do you know anyone that might do that?"

"I think I have just the man for you. Let me speak to him and I'll see what he says. Where are you going now?" Juan asked.

"I need a decent hotel, safe, clean, not too expensive."

"Follow me, I know the place."

We left the airport, got a cab and I was led to a tidy three star hotel, which looked suitable. While Juan went in search of my request, I got a room and cleaned up. About two hours later, my 'guide' returned, with a slightly dejected look on his face.

"Well?"

"I talked to the Captain, and he said he'd do it, but he wants one-hundred and fifty dollars per day. I couldn't get him to do it for any less." Then Juan' eyes brightened up as he added, "But he said for that price he'll supply the food, water, cook and even pay me."

"Sounds good to me. Take me to your Captain," I kidded.

We made our way through the throng of people at the wharf, onto the dock and straight up to a double-decker red and white 'African Queen' style boat. Captain Jorge immediately welcomed us onboard. I quickly took a liking to this jovial soul, and since he too spoke Spanish, we were able to quickly pound out a deal. For the money I was putting up, he would pay Juan as a guide, supply a cook, food and water. We reached an agreement for a four-day excursion to depart the next day. Of course, he needed money to buy supplies, so I paid him upfront, which normally is a real no-no in these countries. But my intuition said do it and that was that.

I then set off to buy a camera. Manaus is a duty free port and people come from all over South America to buy cameras, computers and other electronic gadgets for a good price. I found the camera I was looking for, made a deal, but when I went to pay for it, I discovered that my Visa was maxed out. Fortunately, I had paid for the voyage, and had money to pay the hotel and food, but that was about it! I made a quick call to Canada and had a friend take some money from my account and put it on my Visa. It would take a couple of days before this would be available, but I wouldn't need money where I was going anyhow. But of course there was the matter of the camera.

"I have a bit of a problem," I told Captain Jorge. "I have no camera and I sure would like to have some pictures of this trip."

"I have a video camera and a 35 mm you can use. Please share the photos with me so that I can use them advertising my business," he countered.

This worked out great for me, so we made ready to cast off at dawn.

Chapter 13

As we pushed out into the relatively slow waters of the Rio Negro, we headed downstream to where the muddy Rio Solimoes meets the clear black Rio Negro. According to Brazilian maps, this is where the real Amazon begins. North American maps call the Rio Solimoes the Amazon, which originates in Peru. We headed out into the convergence of these two mighty rivers – what a sight to see – this brown mass of dirty water from the South West meeting the black waters arriving from the North West. At this point, there was a large diversity of fish, so dolphins were engaged in a delightful feast, leaping out of the water all around us. The Rio Negro temporarily halts its journey at this point, forming an almost lake-like setting, as the impact of the large Rio Solimoes creates a water wall. The two rivers flow side by side for many miles downstream, before they finally blend as one.

After fuelling up at a floating 'gas station', and acquiring a large amount of ice, we headed upstream. My home for the next few days consisted of a main deck with a table and benches. The helm was towards the rear and beside this was a small bathroom. The galley was at the stern, with a small platform to stand on. The motor compartment was below deck and our power came from a chugging four-cylinder Duestch motor. The upper deck proved to be an ideal spot to absorb the sun and surroundings. We slung our hammocks on the main deck, providing us a very comfortable place to retire; that is, when wrapped with mosquito netting.

It was difficult to persuade the captain to avoid the tourist traps, so for the first day, that's where we ended up. However, we did visit a couple of interesting places. Heading up the Solimoes, we pulled into a floating zoo of sorts. The people had a large alligator, a couple of sloths, some Macaws and parrots, all of which they liked to display – for a fee. It was interesting, but not what I was seeking.

We then headed into channels of water that flowed between the two large rivers; this water was mainly from the clean and dark Rio Negro. We chugged slowly upstream, passing by the homes of the innovative Amazonians. There were houses floating on logs, while others stood out of the water on stilts. Some of the stilted homes had watermarks half way up the walls, testimony that in some years the water rose even higher than they expected. Cattle foraged on islands, some of these being man-made. Everywhere clothes were either being washed or hung out to dry. I had to wonder what the women did before the missionaries came and insisted they all wear clothes. The washing of clothes seemed to be a bit of a social event, with children splashing about in the water, while the women visited with one another as they scrubbed away.

"Do you want to catch an alligator, Ron?"

"I don't think so Juan."

"Really, we can do it tonight. We're going to tie up soon at a friend's house. We can then go fishing for some piranha, take a swim and then canoe into the lagoon later tonight. I'll show you something amazing."

"Well, I'm game for just about anything, but think I'll pass on the swimming." I said this in all seriousness. Even though I had seen people go in and out of the water without incident, mental images of the sharp-toothed piranhas gobbling up some white meat encouraged me to remain a land lubber. This vision intensified the moment we took a canoe into the jungle and I started catching those feisty little red-gilled fish. Once on the hook, and suspended out of the water, their teeth chattered on the metal hook, echoing throughout the trees. This was a smaller variety of piranha, but they schooled together, blood being an immediate attraction for them. I tossed a chunk of meat into the lagoon and the water began to boil as the furious fish schooled in to devour it. And Juan wanted me to go for a swim here? Not too likely. Back on the boat, while others went for a swim, I took time to absorb my surroundings. The people were very relaxed and our intrusion did not seem to concern them. Full of laughter and joy, they could find humour in the smallest of occurrences (and I knew I was the brunt of some of this). Sadly, I did not understand the language, so I could not retaliate or join in. As the sun sank in the western sky, the frogs began to croak and the sound soon drowned out all other noises of the night. I shone my flashlight along the river's surface and spotted some snakes wiggling their way upstream. I was grateful they were swimming away, and not towards the boat and me.

"Well, are you ready to go?" asked Juan.

"Where?"

"To catch some alligators."

"Are you serious?" I couldn't believe he really meant it.

"Yes, come on, you'll love it. Just bring your flashlight."

Off we went, paddling in a little dugout canoe into the dark night. These small boats, carved from hardwood trees, sat very low in the water. Only about three inches separated me from the hungry fish and reptiles waiting below. I tried very hard not to make any fast or unnecessary moves. We canoed through the canopy of trees using the flashlight to guide us. We finally came out into a clearing, a temporary swamp formed by the high water from the river. The absence of the moon allowed the stars to display their infinite splendour. The sounds of frogs, birds and other exotic noises created a mystical symphony that added to this magical moment.

"Take your flashlight and shine it around," requested Juan. "Look for some red eyes." A few moments passed.

"I see some! Look… there…to your right." I whispered excitedly.

"I see them. Paddle slowly toward them. Keep the flashlight steady on the eyes." This wasn't all that easy; I had to hold the flashlight in my mouth, while slowly paddling and following its quivering beam of light.

As we approached the alligator, Juan gradually got onto his knees, leaned over the front and dipped his hands into the water. There was a splash, and he came up empty handed.

"Got away, let's find another," whispered Juan.

Soon we did spot another, and went through the same routine, with an equal result.

"There, to your left," I directed Juan as I shone the light on a pair of glowing, red rubies in the still, black water.

We slowly made our way forward, Juan kneeling and poised for the capture. Suddenly he yelled,

"Back up, back up; quick, it's a big one."

This amplified the flow of adrenalin tenfold, allowing me to back-paddle with un-natural ferocity.

"A little too big to bring in the canoe," laughed Juan.

About this time, I was ready to call it a night, but Juan insisted we try once more. It wasn't long before we spied another pair of beady, red eyes, beckoning us into the darkness. We went through the same routine as before, but this time Juan was successful. He scooped the small alligator out of the water, grasping him behind the front legs. Juan flopped the foot long reptile onto its back and into the bottom of the canoe. What he did next caught me by surprise; Juan started petting the alligator's belly. The animal quickly became very docile, his sharp teeth no longer presenting a major hazard. After we both had a chance to savour the conquest, we returned the small beast to the water.

"Now it's your turn Ron."

"No thanks, I think that's enough excitement for one night. Let's head back now."

Once we got back on the big boat, I wasted no time in crawling into my hammock. It had been one long and exciting day. Even the incessant croaking of the frogs did not prevent me from finding the solace of sleep.

The following day we made our way through some narrow channels over to the Rio Negro. There we encountered hills, banks and visible land. We explored some tributaries as far as the depth and width of the river would allow our big boat. It was while up one of these that I had another brainchild.

"Juan, would you talk to the people in that hut and see if I can rent their canoe?"

"Where do you want to go?" he asked.

"Just want to go do some stress relief, paddle about for a couple of hours."

Thus, I ended up renting a dugout canoe from the natives, told my crew I wanted some solitude and paddled off alone. The comments I later heard on the video camera revealed just how crazy they thought this Canadian was.

Out in the river, alone and savouring the moment, my serenity was soon dashed when a loud whooshing sound came from behind me. I quickly turned to see a curious, grey dolphin inspecting this strange spectacle in his domain. Another one appeared directly in front of me, but this one was pink. Visions of becoming their 'beach ball' persuaded me to paddle frantically for the safety of the waterlogged jungle. As I peered out at my antagonists from the safety of the forest, I started to chuckle aloud. I had to be the only person ever to scurry into the jungle to escape being potentially tossed about by a dolphin.

Back on the boat, I made another unusual request.

"I want to find a native to guide us into the jungle and spend a night there."

"Are you crazy?" Juan exclaimed.

"No, I'm serious. These people do it all the time, so there's no reason why, with them guiding, we can't."

Juan was quite hesitant, as he quickly realized he would have to follow along on this caper, if for no other reason than to be my interpreter. With some good-natured bantering, I managed to persuade him to join me. We paddled off in the borrowed canoe, up the narrow tributary, looking for a guide. We discovered a small village, one side of which extended to the tributary, the other on the banks of the big river. The subsequent visit with these people left me emotionally distraught for the rest of my holiday.

We convinced an elder to share the story of his people with us. One thing that astonished me was how the old man shared their sad history without rancour. I, on the other hand, was left with many negative feeling resonating inside me.

Ten years earlier, this tribe had lived in the jungle as hunters and fishermen. They lived off the bounty the forest provided, worshipped Mother Earth and lived a contented life. Then the missionaries arrived. They informed the natives that it was uncivilized to run around naked, their spiritual beliefs were pagan and they needed to become agriculturalists. Therefore, they moved out of the jungle to this location, planted yucca and caught fish, not only to eat, but also to sell. Money, which was not required before, now became a necessity in order to buy clothes and donate to the church.

I looked about the tiny settlement and I did not see lush crops nor any smiling faces. These well-dressed people now toiled with the infertile soil, attempting to grow enough food to eat. From my stance, I felt the church should have been donating to these people, not coming in once a week to give a service and take ten per cent of their paltry earnings. Whenever the Bible was mentioned, he always seemed to speak in one way or another of the importance of this contribution. I had to work very hard at keeping my mouth shut, listening and not displaying my true sentiment about what he was sharing. He seemed to have accepted life as it now was. Maybe I could have learned something from the elder about acceptance. I thanked the old gentleman, and gave him some 'money' for his time, further contaminating an old way of life which was fast disappearing.

We returned to the big boat and found the guide had now returned to the settlement. He invited us into his small hut, and I couldn't help but note the only item hanging on its barren walls – a picture of Jesus. Still weighed down heavily from our visit in the village, I was not in a very positive frame of mind regarding such matters. Thankfully, the language barrier prevented me from getting too personal about my observations. The Indian guide agreed to take us to an area in the jungle where he hunted.

Early in the morning we struck out in the canoe. We paddled up a narrow stream until we found the entrance to a path barely visible to the naked eye. We then set off on a two-hour hike along this veiled pathway. I have to admit that at first I was slightly disappointed. On this short jaunt, I expected to see all the beauty National Geographic had spent years to capture on film. Colour did not abound; green dominated the scene. I was not tripping over snakes on the trail, nor encountering any wild jaguars. One absence that I really noticed was that of odour. My sense of smell has always been quite keen, and here there did not seem to be any, other than fresh, clean air. My initial let down soon dissolved, as I gradually digested the uniqueness of the moment. We travelled light; I carried my hammock and the native guide carried a shotgun and a small can, contents of which were unknown to me. Juan packed in the grub.

Upon arriving in the clearing that our guide had in mind, we all became elated to see two large monkeys, high up in the trees. Our guide quickly brought his shotgun to his shoulder and shot one of them. However, the dead monkey did not tumble out of the tree as expected. It caught up in the branches, causing us to spend our first hour chopping the tree down with a machete to retrieve his prize. The guide informed us that there was enough meat in this one animal to feed his whole family. For this reason, he did not skin it, nor would he share its meat with us. This was quite a large mammal, about the size of a chimpanzee. The guide made a papoose affair out of vines and used this to transport his catch home.

We formed a triangle by using one tree and two posts, which were hand pounded into the soft ground as supports for our hammocks. We lit a campfire and prepared our meal of rice and beans. Now it came time for the campfire stories, with Juan once again interpreting. One of these stories shared was of 'ruthless attack monkeys', the obvious intent being to install fear in this crazy Canuck.

"So, what's in the can?" I asked.

Juan repeated my question to the guide who responded in Portuguese.

"This is a can of diesel that I burn all night to keep the Jaguars away. I've had a lot of trouble around my house with them and there are quite a few around here."

I was shocked by this response. This man possessed all the confidence in the world, not to mention a very large gun. At least now, I too could sleep more confidently, although I would have to keep one eye open for those 'attack monkeys'. Maybe, like the jaguars, they too were scared of the light. The hike, the peace and orchestra of jungle sounds were cause for me to fall asleep faster than I anticipated.

Departing the next day, I had a deep sense of satisfaction. One burning desire had just been resolved, and although it had not turned out to be what I expected, the jungle trek definitely quelled an old yearning. I had travelled into the jungle to a place few, if any, white men had gone before, experiencing the virgin forest in its truly natural state. Thanking the guide upon our return for this unforgettable trip, I gave him my small Mag-lite flashlight to help him keep those big cats at bay – and maybe even those attack-monkeys.

We slowly made our way down river to Manaus. I spent hours on the rear platform, contemplating all that I had seen. I could not rid myself of the anguish ingrained in my heart during the visit with the old man in the village. I almost felt compelled to return to North America and go on my own crusade to ban missionaries from these lands. As time went on, I was to meet some very kind missionaries, who were learning from, as well as helping, these very trusting and innocent persons. I have since had to re-evaluate my initial judgements.

Once back in Manaus, I visited the market, which rivalled the one I experienced in Georgetown. Contrasts, such as large dugout canoes laden with bananas on their thatched roofs, parked beside the yachts of the rich townsfolk caught my attention. Pigs, chickens, ducks and other forms of livestock arrived by boat, all of which were to be butchered and sold in the market. Fruits, vegetables and other plants added to the flavour of the market. Of course, there was the ever- present variety of fish. My nasal senses were overwhelmed by the contrasting smells.

I left Manaus and flew back to Rio, where I spent a couple of days on the Copacabana. My summation of this city (by what I saw in this brief period) is that it is truly a city of extreme contrasts. The wind surfers were flying along the coastline, while the subway surfers were dangerously riding the tops of subway cars, ducking and jumping past wires. At nine in the morning health fanatics dominated the walkway on the Copacabana, by nine in the evening it was the domain of prostitutes. Two blocks back from the Ritzy restaurants and hotels on the beachfront, was a world of poverty. Well-dressed teens laughing and having a great time on the beach were in stark contrast to the young urchins hassling tourists for something to eat, just across the street. The police killed ten of these street kids when I was there; this made world headlines, as they normally only shot one or two a day.

A lovely girl named Natalie became my guide for these two days, and showed me sights normal tourists did not experience. She explained the difference between Black Magic and Good Magic. It was truly a haunting city. This is the 'Rio de Janeiro' that became fixed in my memory.

How could I anticipate, while flying back to Caracas, that the concrete jungle had far more for me to fear than anything I had just experienced in the depths of the rainforest.

Chapter 14

WEEKEND HOMICIDE STATISTICS announced every Monday morning an average of twenty-five murders. Venezuela only had a population of twenty-five million, which made these weekly killing sprees even more appalling. These were normally the settling of scores, or were perpetrated by the police shooting those reportedly 'resisting arrest'. The Government discontinued this practice in 2003, when the numbers averaged eighty to one-hundred murders for this three-day period. On my return from Brazil, I came very close to adding to this statistic. The stress that I had discarded on the big river to the south was about to be quickly replaced.

Fred requested that I come to the company apartment to arrange for the return to El Dividivi. He had bought a new Toyota pickup that I was to drive there, while he and Ciro would follow along in the company car.

"Ron, take these keys and go for a drive in the new truck to make sure it has no problems. I know you don't like driving in this crazy city, but you're going to have to get used to it sometime. Traffic shouldn't be too bad at this time of night," Fred ensured.

"Ok," I replied, "where do I find this truck, and what colour is it?"

"Next door in the parking lot. There's no room for it in our compound. It's blue and fully loaded. Air conditioning, stereo, the works. You'll like it."

I stepped outside to find my new set of wheels. In the poorly lit parking lot next door, the only truck that fit the description had someone in it. It took a moment to realize that the person was in my new, blue Toyota! I approached the vehicle, glanced inside and observed a fellow bent down feverishly dismantling the steering column. I swung the door open and harshly demanded,

"Que pasa?"

Surprised, the man jerked his head up sharply, and then looked at me incredulously as if to inquire, 'who the hell are you?'

This caused me to hesitate for a moment, second-guessing myself, but seeing his tools reinforced that I was not the intruder. My years of training at the gaol instantly kicked in; my previously sharp awareness skills did not. This nearly cost me my life.

I pulled the man out of the truck and pinned him against the box of the pickup. He was quite tall for a Venezuelan, over six feet, so I had my hands full. His one hand remained behind his back, and I presumed that it held either a knife or a screwdriver. Now that I had him restrained, I needed help. All apartment blocks in that area had armed security guards, normally dressed in plain clothes. I yelled out desperately, hoping one of them would come to my assistance.

A man appeared and I shouted at him,

"Llama la policia!"

He stared at me inquisitively, and I repeated my demand to call the police.

This stranger then slowly started circling around behind me, not saying a word. Suddenly out of nowhere came a short, stocky, moustached man brandishing a pistol in his left hand. As he ran into this bizarre scene, he was yelling and directing his attention at the thief I had constrained. This led me to believe that he was indeed one of the local security guards, and with this assumption came newfound bravado. My Spanish curses flowed as freely as the adrenalin in my body. Abruptly, the stocky man turned and placed the barrel of the pistol inches from my forehead.

"Cállese," he said, motioning me to back off and telling me to shut up.

I released my hold on the thief and retreated, but my mouth didn't cease its verbal onslaught. I thought my old axiom of a good defence being a good offence was at play; in reality, I was experiencing a moment of insanity.

What happened next, and what logically should have happened did not correlate. In a land where life was cheap, a quick bullet to my head would have ended my incessant chatter. The keys and money in my pocket would be theirs for the taking; there were no witnesses and all they had to do was fling my lifeless body into the gutter. Yes, the outcome should have been obvious.

What did transpire puzzled me. The man with the gun pointed at my head, slowly lowered his pistol, turned and sauntered away with the other two men. As they strolled off down the street, I overheard the stocky one scolding the car thief. He was berating him for being too slow, getting caught and causing all of them to blow their cover.

As my protective adrenalin receded, reality slowly set in and sanity returned. My legs started to shake. The fact that I had clearly seen all three of their faces did not seem to bother them one bit. That had to be my saving grace!

Incredibly, at this time Fred drove out of the compound. The three banditos were still visible far down the street. His response was that I should continue with my drive. I was very shook up, but after arguing with him for a bit, I did as he suggested. Although the wires had been exposed beneath the steering column, the truck did start without any problem. The odometer was a different story. Broken, it registered eight point five kilometres from then on.

As I set forth on my tour of Caracas, I now had time to reflect on what had just occurred. The most predominant question in my mind was, 'why had they let me go?' No doubt, God had intervened, that was incontestable. Maybe them expecting a scared victim and getting a 'loco' gringo instead, was the safe passage He provided. All I knew was that I was very lucky to be alive. Still quite rattled, I ended up taking a wrong turn. I found myself in the ghetto district that was a virtual no-mans land, one not entered by anyone other than those who lived there. Somehow, I managed to turn around and find my way out, heading straight for the apartment. That was enough close encounters for one night. I double-parked the truck in our apartment's compound, and called it a night.

The next morning, Ciro true to form, was late as usual. About nine am there was a knock at the door. A young lad asked us to move the truck, since his mother could not get her car out. I moved the truck back to the parking lot next door. Normality prevailed on this typical Saturday morning, with two children playing with a wagon, a man cutting his lawn and neighbours chatting with each other. I parked the truck and returned to the apartment.

From our apartment window I maintained vigilance, strolling to the window every five minutes or so to ensure all was normal. At about nine-thirty, and still no sign of Ciro, I once more visited the window.

"Fred, you're not going to believe this," I said.

"What, it's gone?" he asked in disbelief.

"That's right. It's gone!" I exclaimed.

That fast, our truck made its way into the hands of these persistent thieves and no doubt over the border to Columbia. In my two years with the company, we purchased twelve new Toyotas (two cars and ten trucks). Of these, one car and three trucks vanished. Fred had his car scooped right out from under his nose. He watched helplessly from his restaurant patio table as it was driven away with alarms blaring, in the middle of the afternoon!

Ciro eventually arrived, and was met with a hostile audience. Had he been on time, the car thieves would not have had the window of opportunity he had afforded them. To add insult to injury, Ciro had not completed insuring the truck yet, so we could not report it stolen until Monday, after that acquisition was complete.

The three of us then drove ten hours west in Fred's car to El Dividivi. It felt good to be back home where life was actually moving along rather smoothly. Brent's good management techniques had boosted our production, and the project was running in black ink.

The men discovered that Brent was partial to boa constrictors, so we soon had five of these reptiles in a pen in the yard. Feeding them became quite a performance, as they seemed only to have a taste for small rabbits. It became the task of our 'go-fer', Jose, to search out food sources for these critters. Sometimes he would get a rabbit that was too big for their appetite, and the cook ended up having to feed the rabbit in the pen with the snakes, a job that did not overly delight her.

I decided to visit some of the local sights, so I asked Rose if she would mind showing me around. I rented a pickup from one of our workers, and off we went. We climbed up the inside of the forty-six meter high Virgen del la Paz statue in old Valera. What a view from her eyes!

On the way home from this relaxing day we rounded a corner on a very dark highway and encountered a parade of people. They were walking in our lane and carrying candles to light their way. I swerved onto the other side of the highway, barely missing this gathering of men, women and children. The faith of these people knew no bounds, and He certainly protected them that night.

About this time, we commenced another project on the opposite side of the country in Maturin. My position now became one of training and supervising administrators. I had created the spreadsheets that we faxed daily to Canada, outlining our production and expenses incurred. Thus commenced countless airplane trips back and forth across the country, all flights passing through Caracas where plane changes were required. On one of these trips, Fred called me to the office. He took me out for supper, just the two of us. After we had finished the main course, he leaned forward, looked me straight in the eyes and said,

"Adrian is coming down here next week. He wants you to be present. He may be asking you some questions about my expenses down here." Fred's stare became very stern, and menacing. "I'm telling you now, that if you disclose any facts that hurt me, I will return the favour. Do you understand what I'm saying?"

Caught off guard by his sudden change of demeanour, I hesitated with my reply.

"If you hurt me, I'll hurt you?" he clarified. He knew I had been instrumental in having him removed from his luxury hotel and into the apartment that now served as his home and office. He was making certain that I did not disrupt the 'golden goose' once more. What could I say? Although Adrian owned the company, Fred was the boss here, so I replied,

"Don't worry."

Nothing else was said on this matter, and the next day I carried on my way.

A week later, I went to Caracas, and joined an informal meeting with the owner of the company, party managers, and, of course, Fred. He never let me out of his sight. Whenever Adrian started talking to me one on one, Fred would interrupt and lead Adrian away on some other topic. Thus, Adrian departed with his rose-coloured glasses, none the wiser, or so I thought. Shortly thereafter, a female controller arrived in the country, and I once more found myself summoned to the city. This time she was spelling out to me what would happen if my records were not in order. As she appeared to be a very no-nonsense person, I was sure that she would soon expose Fred's indiscretions.

As we prepared to go out for supper, I passed the bedroom on the way to the washroom; lo and behold, there was Fred smooching with our new controller. He was truly one sly guy. Very shortly thereafter, Adrian returned for his second trip to the country and fired them both. He then queried me as to why I had not reported the irregularities to him. I pointed out to him that I sent daily cost reports, and had trusted that he would see the discrepancies. He replied that he had, and that was why he was here. He obviously was more astute than many of us gave him credit for. My friend Brent was elevated to the position of Country Manager, leaving me with the care and control of his pet snakes.

With this turn of events, projects now became more organized and professional. Brent hired a country administrator who spoke English to ensure we followed legal accounting practices, making my position somewhat more complex. I now had to build a rapport with this new individual, which I did without any problem. I soon learned though, that any positive changes that I came up with, he would take the credit for. When he made a mistake, in any which way, it suddenly became my mistake.

With all the time I spent flying, I observed some very out of the ordinary occurrences which one would not likely see flying in North America. Some were comical, others were not. One time a stewardess opened the cockpit door and joked with the pilot just as he hit the throttle. He aborted the takeoff, taxied around and attempted once more to get us into the air. This time, with no interruptions, he was successful. Utilizing the taxi strip to gain speed was another extreme practice. Our wingtips would nearly touch the tarmac each time, as we swung around to line up with the runway. But, there was one particular flight to Maturin that had, not only myself, but all the passengers holding private conversations with the Man upstairs.

Chapter 15

I SETTLED BACK INTO the comfortable seat of the old DC-9 and assumed the position I had become accustomed to. I had learned just how much a ten dollar first class ticket increased my comfort on these frequent flights. This meant no long line-ups for a boarding pass and a lot of extra leg room, so that I could stretch out and go to sleep. And that is just what I did. Before the plane had departed the gate, I was sound asleep.

The descent of the plane awakened me and I peered through sleep-laden eyes at the terrain below. My doziness quickly vanished as I stared at the mountains below – Maturin didn't have mountains! I turned to the passenger at my side and inquired,

"Donde estamos?"

"Cumana. Este avión detiene aquí, entonces va a Maturin." He informed me that this particular flight had an extra stop thrown in, one of which I was unaware. Well, no big deal. At least I knew I hadn't boarded a flight destined completely off my path, like a close friend of mine once did. He'd ended up on an island out in the Caribbean.

The plane did not gently touchdown on the runway, but rather came down hard and bounced high into the air. When the wheels touched the tarmac the second time, I felt relieved to be on the ground. I was wrong! We were catapulted into the air a second time. Now I knew the pilot had lost control, and our next descent was going to be uncontrolled, and hard, with about 98,000 lbs landing on four very small tires. Sure enough, it felt like we had just fallen out of the sky when we touched down again. I was sure the wheel struts would pierce right through the wings. To my amazement, we stayed on the ground this time, without even one tire blown.

Once at the terminal, I watched for mechanics to come and assess if there had been any damage. To my consternation, no one appeared.

"Que pasa?" I asked the stewardess, as passengers were exiting and being replaced by others boarding for our continued flight.

"Nuevo capitán," new co-pilot, she explained.

Once the plane was loaded, we took off without incident. A sense of foreboding pervaded the atmosphere inside the plane. No new passengers had entered first class, and it became deadly silent. Not a soul was talking. Taking a glance around, I realized that most passengers were deep in prayer. Since we had to land once again, on what must be damaged landing gear, I too joined the prayer group, bowed my head and turned my life over to God's care.

We descended into Maturin. With my head down, eyes closed and deep in prayer, I waited for the inevitable. Our relief was truly audible when the plane touched down light as a feather, with not even a bounce.

"Viva capitán," erupted the passengers in unison from all sections of the plane. With that loud proclamation, the pent up fear throughout the aircraft was expelled. It was then that I realized that I wasn't the only one who understood the dynamics of the initial hard landing.

This was just the beginning of a very traumatic day. When I arrived at our work compound, I found the place under siege. Police cars, an ambulance and men blocked the entrance to both our yard and office. The union had decided to go on strike and were now preventing vehicles from entering or leaving through the chain link gate.

I got out of the taxi and made my way around to the back where I was able to gain access.

"What the hell's going on here?"

"The workers refused to work this morning. They want more money, same old, same old. But now that's the least of our problems. Joe took it upon himself to crash through the gate with the Toyota. Some of the workers were hurt but we don't know how bad. The thing is, now we have to find Joe and get him out of the country. The police are involved and this could get real serious," the Project Manager informed me.

"Have you got a vehicle on the outside, back at the house or somewhere?" I asked.

"Ya, but kind of hard getting over there right now," he chuckled.

"I'll hold the fort here, if you want to sneak out the way I got in. Grab a cab and do what you have to. Down here, as a gringo, nothing's fair, nothing's just and we have no rights. We have to take care of our own."

So off went the Project Manager, while Hector (our Maturin administrator) and I attempted to quell the rising tide of anger outside our gate. Eventually the Venezuelan managers (of the main contractor) were able to settle things down. They deferred the police, for the time being, which allowed us time to find Joe and whisk him out of the country back to Canada. Joe had not learned that there were certain things one did not do in a foreign country and the consequences for him would have been a magnified ten fold because he was an "extranjero". The luxuries of a Canadian prison would be a far cry from the housing he would receive in this land!

The men returned to work the following day; no one was seriously hurt and life returned to normal. Once I had fulfilled my purpose, I wasted no time returning to the other side of the country. The workers we had there were far more conciliatory.

With American Thanksgiving coming on, my U.S. compatriots insisted we find a turkey and do it up right. We sent Jose off again, this time to find food for us, instead of the snakes. He returned with a tough looking old Tom that had us in stitches.

"That bird's no good," I cautioned Jose.

"No problemo, mira," he replied.

Jose told us not to worry, as he knew how to tenderize this bird.

He pulled a bottle out of his pocket and proceeded to force feed the turkey a good dose of rum. We gathered about, not believing Jose was serious. He persisted until the turkey could no longer walk, and then butchered it. Although the rum did not tenderize the wings, the rest of the turkey did provide us with the Thanksgiving feast we desired. I later found out that this practice is quite commonplace in this part of the country. So, instead of a stuffed turkey, we ended up with a sloshed one. No wonder the local beef was so tough; they certainly couldn't afford this procedure with an animal that size!

After this exciting year, it now came time to take a real break and go home for Christmas. I made the adjustment from the intense heat to the immense cold without too much difficulty. After taking in some twelve-Step meetings, I felt peace settle in once more. Adventure had its costs. After a nice festive visit with my family, it was off to the ski slopes of Big Mountain, Montana with my son. With family ties reconnected and a renewed calm, I found myself once more on a plane returning south to my foreign home.

I was greeted with a surprise birthday party on my return to Venezuela, making the welcome back complete. There was even a rare little earth tremor my first night 'home', although I'm sure I didn't cause it. The staff informed me that the snakes had to go. They were tired of caring for them and the dangers they presented. I took the boas out back and turned them loose into the wild from which they came. No doubt, they appreciated it as much as the cooks did.

All good things must come to an end, and thus it was with that project. We now moved into the state of Zulia, and hired a new crew chosen from seven different unions. Now the real adversity began! We moved into the oldest oil site in Venezuela, Mene Grande. The original production oil well in Venezuela was still pumping away. Oil literally flows on the surface of the ground in some locations, with small fires burning on some portions. The workers in this area had years of experience making sure their family had continuous employment. Our focus on production now disrupted that agenda. We became the enemy, and they now implemented every means at their disposal, imaginable and unimaginable, to remove this foreign company from their soil. I became their first target. One day four people stormed my office and started rattling things off in Spanish, much faster than I could comprehend. I just kept saying, 'Si, si', hoping they would just go away. I presumed that one was a safety person and another was from the union. I didn't have a clue who the other two were. After I had answered 'yes' numerous times to their questions, they departed as quickly as they had arrived.

Later in the day, the Contract Manager informed me that I could no longer remain on the site. There was no letter of reprimand, no chance to explain, no recourse. The union demanded that I leave immediately. When I had been saying si, si, si, I had been saying yes, I had bribed the Police Captain, yes, I had bribed the Commandant and yes to a host of other incriminating actions. The reason for this set up was that I had discovered we were paying many employees who were not even working for us and they did not want me uncovering their scam. One down, rest of the company to go.

Glad to be out of that part of the country, I moved my meagre belongings over to another project we had under way on the Columbian border in a place called Machiques. Here I soon encountered problems of another sort. I convinced the main contractor that I knew what I was doing regarding a particular computer program, and ended up crashing our computer and theirs as well. I was in a real quandary, and two days of attempting to repair the problem had me stressed to the limit, as well as all others involved. All data such as employees, work progress and a host of other facts, were now inaccessible. There was a very strong chance we were about to loose this contract over my carelessness. It seemed that only a miracle would get me out of this mess.

And, arrive it did! It began with a knock at the door at two in the afternoon. This was an uncommon occurrence during siesta time, since this was an unofficial local time-out. I approached the door hesitantly. Living on the Columbian border one did have to be cautious. I peered out the window and observed a Caucasian man standing at our door.

"Can I help you?" I inquired, as I opened the door.

"I sure hope so. I am looking for the Occidental Oil Company, which is in this area somewhere."

"You're on the right highway, they're just a few miles further south," I replied.

"Good, thanks a lot. I've come down here from New York to repair some kind of computer problem they have."

With a miracle staring me in the face, I wasn't about to let it dissipate. I dragged him inside and pleaded with him to help me with my current dilemma. Two hours later, not only had he fixed my computer, but the contractor's as well. With such a Positive nudge, I was once more very conscious of God's presence in my life.

After taking a short scuba diving break in Curacao, I met up with my old friend Albert in Caracas. We had lots to catch up on, and of course, there was the never-ending gold-en opportunities waiting if one were to catch onto Albert's dreams. He introduced me to a woman that was to awaken a slumbering a dream of my own. The hassles and stress in the oil industry were taking their toll on me; I was ripe for other options. Perhaps tourism was the answer.

Yvette, like Albert, was from Trinidad. She had a Muslim background and was presently steering tourists to local full-fledged tour companies for a commission. I felt she could do better than that. We shortly became not only partners in a business venture, but also in life as well. We set out to build working relationships with tour companies all over the country. This not only took me to places most people never get to see, but onto new adventures as well. One of the first such journeys was to that supposed idyllic, deserted, Tropical Island of every man's fantasy. Some dreams are best left in the mind, as I was soon to find out.

Chapter 16

U PON ARRIVAL IN Chichiriviche, about three hours west of Caracas, Venezuela, I set out to fulfil one of my lifelong fantasies. My intent was to spend a delightful night on a secluded and deserted island with my beautiful girlfriend, Yvette. This dashing, young lady with short-cropped hair and East-Indian features, was as excited about this as I was. Originally from Trinidad, she now made Venezuela her home, but had never ventured to this part of the country. We had been going together for several months and decided it was time to take a break from the noise of the big city.

As we stood on the beach looking at the islands offshore, it was readily apparent which ones received heavy use. With no desire to join the swarms of people, I peered out over the Caribbean searching for another option. There, in the distant north, I observed a speck on the horizon. I asked a local fisherman what the name of that island was.

"Cayo Borracho. Usted no quiere ir allí."

Of course, telling me that I didn't want to go there aroused my curiosity.

"Por que?" I asked.

"Hay bastante ratons allí. Y el agua esta furioso a veces. Tambien, esta muy lejos."

It has been noted that I have a bad habit of nodding my head in agreement as if I understand everything said, when in fact I don't.

Here I did it again. The fisherman talked too fast for me to understand, and my pride prevented me from asking Yvette to interpret. I'd soon find out exactly what he had said – the hard way.

And so we struck a deal for conveyance to the island, and purchased food and water for two days. We set forth in his small skiff for Cayo Borracho, interpreted into English, 'Drunk Island'. Three hours later, we set foot on our tropical isle. Now I understood part of the fisherman's warning. The water was rough, and yes, it was a long ways to the mainland. With a look of uncertainty, our captain departed, leaving us to fend for ourselves for the next twenty-four hours, providing the sea permitted his return.

Fantasy Island – here I stood at last, alone with my girlfriend and no one about to disturb the solitude. We quickly shed our clothes and took to the water, snorkelling about the beautiful coral that ran adjacent to the shoreline. Engulfed in this underwater paradise, I ventured away from the shore, and my partner, following the multitude of colourful fish as they flitted to and fro.

On the bottom, curled beneath a piece of coral, I observed what appeared to be an eel. I ventured closer, and as the water was quite shallow, I did not need to dive down for a better look. A previous visit to the underwater aquarium in Curacao had educated me on many forms of aquatic life. What I saw now caused me immediate alarm. This was no eel, but the famed sea snake, an elusive and not often observed ocean resident. I could not believe my eyes and moved even closer to make sure I was not mistaken. This highly venomous serpent took exception to this and came forth to greet me. About face and flippers in full gear, I splashed my way toward the now distant shore, expecting at any moment to receive a lethal dose of venom from this agitated creature. Fear, that great protector, propelled me like never before, and in no time, I pulled myself onto the beach.

However, I found I could not walk. My legs cramped up severely from this heavy exertion and it was some time before I rid myself of the excruciating pain in my calves. This put a damper on any further underwater exploration, as I was not about to contest the snake's domain anymore.

"That was a close call, Yvette. Obviously, no one ever comes out here because those snakes don't like visitors."

"Well, maybe it's time we set up camp and have a bite to eat, we'll leave the water life alone," she replied. "I wasn't too comfortable out there myself, especially when you took off for the horizon."

We hung our single hammock between two windblown palms, made a snack and fought the unremitting wind in our attempt to organize our modest campsite. We then made our way to the beach, au natural, to relax and take in the sun. After the earlier excitement, I was now able to relax and allow myself to drift into a meditative state. With the wind caressing my body and blowing in my hair, I was soon lulled into a state of peace that is often hard to attain.

"Hola."

Startled, I came out of my reverie, turned, and observed a young man approaching us about thirty yards away. Too late now for modesty, I simply responded,

"Hola."

Yvette was too shocked to do anything but stare at him.

"Where did you come from?"

"I'm camped on the other side of the island. Heard your boat come in a while ago, so I thought I would drop over and see who'd joined me out here. My name is Franco," he said as he sat down beside us on the sand, seeming oblivious to our non-attire.

Still quite stunned by this intrusion, I asked Franco how long he'd been out here.

"I've been here for a week already. It's been remarkable! I'm from France, and wanted to see what being alone on an island would be like, so here I am."

"Well, sorry we disturbed you. We're looking for the same thing."

"No problem, this island is big enough for all of us. My camp is over there, in the far corner, less wind," Franco said, pointing to the southeast.

We made small talk for about an hour, and then Franco returned to his side of the island, leaving us once more in privacy. The lonely planet does not seem to be very lonely anymore, even in this remote setting. Although his intrusion had upset the tranquility considerably, I was determined not to let it undermine the purpose of this retreat. Unfortunately, snakes and people have a way of messing with my serenity.

As the sun slowly ebbed in the western sky, so did my anxiety. But not for long.

"Did you see that?" I asked Yvette, pointing to a movement on the beach.

"Yes, but I don't know what it is. It's getting dark."

I returned to the campsite and retrieved my flashlight. With my senses heightened, I shone the light into the darkness, looking for movement. Soon a pair of red eyes glared back at me; now the other warning from the fisherman became apparent. Rats! They were all over, scurrying about the sand and not intimidated by our presence at all. One in particular was quite brave, coming right up to my foot, at which time I shooed him away. Rats were the last thing I expected this many miles from the mainland. As darkness settled in, more and more of these little beasts made their presence known.

We returned to our campsite and discovered that the vermin had taken over. Like a scene from the movie 'Willard', they were everywhere, attempting to get into our food and scampering all about. We set about roping our food up into a tree and securing things as best we could. The wind had not receded and this added to the turmoil.

Finally, with nothing else to do but let the rodents take reign, we attempted a feat bordering on the impossible – two persons sleeping in one hammock. After much re-positioning, it appeared that sleep might actually be possible. With the wind blowing the hammock to and fro, we felt ourselves being rocked to sleep.

"Ouch!" I screamed.

"What," replied a startled Yvette?

"I just got bit in the ass by one of those rats. We can't stay like this. We'll have to see if we can get the hammock higher in the trees."

In the darkness, with the furry creatures running all around us, over our feet and up the trees, we managed to raise the hammock to an elevation that did in fact prevent further attacks. Sleep, regrettably, was not fast in coming, nor was the dawn.

Bidding farewell to our 'Tropical Paradise' the following day was not difficult. We concluded that to stay on Cayo Borracho, the 'Drunk Island', one would truly need to be inebriated. The relentless wind, poisonous snake, neighbourly Franco and hordes of rats had not been figured into the equation of my perfect fantasy.

We returned to Caracas and I once more resumed my flights back and forth across the country, coordinating administrative affairs. Yvette continued to recruit tourists for local companies, but was having difficulty interesting anyone in Chichiriviche. I was soon ready for another break and decided to head south into the state of Amazonas. My vision was to organize some kind of tourist facility there. This time I travelled alone, with my camera as my only companion.

I arrived in the humid city of Puerto Ayacucho on the banks of the Orinoco River. With Columbia and its irrepressible rebels just across the river, Venezuela had established a large military presence in the area. Navy, army, guardia and air force, as well as police, made for a slightly intimidating atmosphere. From this city, no movement further south or east into the jungle was allowed without approval from the governor.

Not one to always abide by protocol, I endeavoured to rent a small plane. My plan was to fly into Tama Tama, deep in the heart of Yanomami territory. Situated on the headwaters of the Orinoco, this was not an area normally visited by outsiders.

The pilot assumed I had my paperwork in order, so he agreed to fly me into the forbidden territory. Anthropologists, missionaries and the Guardia National were the only persons normally permitted into this remote region. I walked out onto the tarmac to board the Cessna I had rented. A Sergeant with the Guardia intercepted me.

"Donde vas?"

"Tama Tama."

"Sus papels, por favour?"

"No tengo."

Once I told him I didn't have any papers for my intended flight into the jungle, he informed me that I would not be able to go. I attempted to bribe him, but he recoiled, fearing someone would observe this indiscretion.

"But," he said in Spanish, "if you will let my two soldiers over there accompany you, I will let you go. They need to go in and relieve the two soldiers that are on duty at Tama Tama right now."

"I don't intend to flight directly there, so we'll take longer getting there than normal and will be flying quite low at times. Maybe around fifteen-hundred feet. If they have no problem with that, ok."

The pilot protested about this intrusion, but was also accustomed to this freeloading lot, so he reluctantly agreed. We took off, flew up and over a low mountain range, and then down the other side following the Venturi River. My camera was clicking constantly as I attempted to capture the serpentine river below. I wanted to study the photos later to help me to decide what area would be best for a jungle camp. We zigzagged our way across this immense expanse of uninhabited land and finally landed on a small grass strip in the jungle.

While the two soldiers departed the plane with their guns and equipment, I noticed two others approaching the plane.

"Vaya," I commanded the pilot.

"Are you certain?" he queried in his native tongue.

"Si, go, go, now."

With that, the pilot gunned the engine in his plane, shot down the short runway and took off.

The soldiers started running when they seen the plane taking off, but by the time they arrived where I stood, they were too late. Their anticipated ride out to civilization was gone.

"Where are your papers?" they demanded of me in staccato Spanish.

"I don't have any. I talked to your sergeant and he said I could come in here if I gave your friends a lift in. I want to take a 'bongo' down river back to Puerto Ayacucho," I informed them in my rustic Spanish.

"That's not possible. You need permission."

"Well then, please get it for me."

As we walked towards their compound, the heat and humidity started to assail me with force. By the time we arrived at their hut, I was dying of thirst. Once they accepted the fact that I was not about to call the plane back, they reluctantly attempted to contact the governor by satellite phone to obtain the required permission. While waiting, they provided me with food and much-needed water. They then allowed me to stroll about the tiny settlement.

A young Yanomami child, about six years old, quickly joined me, and I graciously accepted him as my guide. He pointed out where he lived in one of the few small clay huts visible. There was also a small clay hut store, which was closed at this time of day. We continued walking along and soon came to a large complex of white, clapboard buildings. I noted two, young, blonde haired children playing football on the well-manicured lawn. A ride-on lawn mower rested alongside a motorbike against the side of one shed. This struck me as very odd, as there were no roads here, only paths, and the whole length of the settlement, including the guardia station, could not be more than two kilometres.

"Who lives there?' I asked my little guide.

"The missionaries."

"Have you ever been in that big house there?" I asked.

"No, no, certainly not." he exclaimed in his broken Spanish.

Unlike most children, this little fellow had few words. He only spoke short sentences when pointing something out, marching forth with his walking stick, as if guiding a gringo was an everyday occurrence. Finally, we encountered another Yanomami, the young lad's uncle. He was not nearly as amicable as his nephew was. When I tried to negotiate a river trip, he reluctantly agreed, demanding an exorbitant fee for his services. I left him to gather up some supplies and I returned to the Guardia station to see how things were progressing with my requisition. They informed me that it had been denied, so now I was in limbo. I informed them of the deal I had made with the Yanomami. The soldiers said okay, but they made if very clear that I was not to go downstream, and especially not to the Casiquiare River, which joined the Rio Negro in Brazil.

"Why are these people so standoffish," I asked.

"Eight months ago a group of Brazilian miners crossed into their land, entered a village and massacred nearly everyone. When we went in, a missionary and a bunch of armed hostile Indians prevented us from going any further. We called the President by satellite phone and only then were we permitted in. The Yanomami had dealt justice to most of the miners themselves, so there wasn't much left for us to do. They blamed us and all outsiders for this incursion, and now are wary when anyone from the outside comes in here."

"They killed the miners?"

"Yes, all but a couple that managed to get away."

'Certainly no lengthy trials with lawyers getting rich here,' I thought.

My prospective guide appeared, all set to go. At the same time, a large, thatch roofed 'bongo' pulled into shore adjacent the compound. The owner of this long, dugout canoe needed gas for his forty horsepower motor so he could continue on to Puerto Ayacucho. Informing him that gas was available, the soldiers also advised him that he would have three passengers. Once again, it seemed I had some Divine intervention helping me along my precarious path. The Yanomami did not seem at all disappointed in losing his tourist to this Venezuelan entrepreneur.

After a good nights sleep, we slipped away from shore at six in the morning. With the throttle of the big motor wide open, we sped downstream. This being the dry season, there were numerous sandy beaches along the way. Observing the small, native villages we passed, there seemed to be a total passivity in all we saw: children playing in the water, men fishing from their little 'curiaras' (motor-less canoes) and women washing clothes on the rocks. At noon, we stopped on a sandbar, had lunch and then carried on. Just before dark, we put into a small village, where the people greeted us amiably. That evening, the entire village and one gringo sat on the riverbank enjoying a marvellous sunset. The only blight on this otherwise ideal setting was my initiation to the puri-puri, the sand fly whose painful bites became a constant source of aggravation. On our first full day on the river, we had not seen one motorized boat, or outsider in this enchanted land.

Our second day again started early, and about midday, we finally started to encounter other vessels. Once Columbia became our western shore there were even more boats plying the river, some of them quite elaborately painted and equipped. We arrived in the city after dark and I made my way to the hotel. There I reflected on how fortunate I had been to see so many miles of untamed wilderness, an opportunity quickly vanishing in this so-called age of advancement.

The incessant yearning for the extraordinary guaranteed this wouldn't be my last visit to the tropical rain forest. I took a time-out to digest what I had just experienced and to catch up on some much-needed sleep. The hammock on the bongo worked fine, but luxuries such as beds and showers are always appreciated that much more after they have been forsaken for a while. In my dreams that evening, there was no hint of the adventures that were to lie ahead of me in the next few days.

Chapter 17

W ELL RESTED, DESPITE the humidity, I set forth to search out a more legal method of returning to the enticing jungle. I walked out of my hotel and was greeted by the heavy presence of police everywhere. What astonished me most were the unsheathed machetes attached to their belts. When I asked locals what was going on, they informed me that a major court decision was coming down regarding the election of the Governor; if the judges decided in a manner unfavourable to the populace, there was the high possibility of riots. If an uprising was going to be settled by machete wielding police, it was definitely time for me to get out of town.

Before long, I found a small tour company that took care of the required permissions and arranged for a three-day trip. They too wanted to leave before trouble erupted, so they wasted no time packing the bongo and getting us on our way.

One reason I'm not partial to taking tours is that it seems there always has to be 'one in the crowd'. This time it was a self-proclaimed Nazi skin-head, who really had no business going anywhere that didn't have a ready source of alcohol. Despite the arrogance of this one person, the rest of us settled in to enjoy the trip up a small tributary of the Orinoco, into the Parque del Tobagán.

Our first stop was to visit a Piaroa village on the banks of the Cuao River. I had informed the guide that I would like to meet a Shaman, if possible, and now had my wish granted. The guide introduced me to the medicine man, then left to join the others strolling about the village.

I sat down on the ground beside the old man in front of his thatched roof hut. "Are you the only Shaman in the village?"

In his broken Spanish, the Shaman explained, "I try to teach sons ways of the Shaman, but they go to town and not interested now. I the last Shaman on this river, and when I go, then who fix people, huh?"

He also described to me some of the local herbal medicines, as well as their usages. However, his number one cure-all was yopo.

"Yopo best medicine here."

"What is it made from?" I inquired.

Pointing a finger towards some large pods hanging from a nearby tree, he attempted to enlighten me. "That seed and bee honey. We dry seeds, mix with honey and bake until hard. Wait, I show you."

He stood and entered his hut, soon returning with a strange looking apparatus in one hand, while his other hand clutched something tight. He sat down beside me once more and opened his hand. In it, he held a small brown cube. My first reaction was, 'Oh my God, that's hashish', for that's exactly what it looked like. Then he showed me the other item. It was a carved out piece of wood, in the shape of a 'Y'. The bottom of the Y was carved into a bowl, and leading into it were two hollowed out stems of this piece of wood.

"We also use yopo when we talk to Spirits," he went on to explain. The old man attempted to explain some of their beliefs to me, but since he often reverted to his native language, I could not grasp all that he said.

"You want to try?" he asked.

I graciously accepted this invitation, expecting an experience similar to a North American spiritual ceremony, such as in a sweat lodge. This would just be another part of my never ending Spiritual Quest.

When we ducked down and entered the Shaman's dark, conical hut, I was surprised at how cool it was inside. The clay walls acted as a good buffer against the mid-day heat. I sat cross-legged in front of the Shaman and took off my tinted glasses so that I could see better in the darkness. I was quiet as he closed his eyes and said some things in his native tongue, which I assumed was his form of prayer. Opening his eyes, he then took a blunt, rounded piece of wood and crushed a portion of the yopo in the bowl.

In blundered the 'skinhead', loudly proclaiming, "I hear there is some dope being had here. I want to try some too."

This guy had absolutely no couth whatsoever, nor any inkling about the spiritual aspect of what was transpiring. However, the old man just calmly told him to sit down beside me. He then handed the yopo pipe to me, told me to put the stem ends into each nostril and inhale. The mention of dope and disruption of the ambience inhibited my actions now. Thus, I only snorted a small portion into my nostrils and passed the pipe back to the Shaman. He reground some more yopo into the bowl and passed the pipe to the recent arrival. After he had snorted all that was in the bowl, he passed the pipe back to the elder, who then partook himself.

I became quite entranced with the whole affair. The Shaman again said some chants and then fell silent. Finally, he signalled it was time to go outside, and when the large crude fellow attempted to stand, he fell over my way and stepped onto my glasses. Fortunately, the lenses were not broken, but the frames were a mess. Once that fellow was out of the hut, the Shaman motioned for me to sit again. We talked a little bit more, and he gave me a fresh cube of yopo.

"Take this with you and use when time right."

His graciousness and calm demeanour brought me back into the positive state of mind that I had prior to the entry of 'Mr. Skinhead'. I thanked the Medicine Man profusely and stepped out into the sunlight. The crew was waiting by the bongo, so I bid farewell to my wise doctor and boarded the boat once more. Settled down inside the large canoe, I now had time to evaluate how I really felt. Mentally, there were no great hallucinations or any such thing, just a calm feeling. However, my muscles started cramping up and this became quite uncomfortable. I resolved, right then and there, that

I would leave further experimentation with this jungle medicine to others more practised.

A short while later we put into shore and unloaded the bongo. This was where we would commence our four-hour hike into the jungle. The guides carried all the food and supplies, so all I had to concern myself with was my hammock contained within my small backpack. That is, until someone yelled,

"Look out Ron, there's a snake!"

Instinctively I leaped backwards, crashing into the person behind me. As the two of us disentangled ourselves, one member of the troop managed to keep her eye on the snake, which had blended right in with jungle floor. She exclaimed,

"There it is. See, right there. Wow! You're lucky. It went right between your legs."

The guide came back and quickly identified the snake as a small Fer de Lance, or in his language, a Mapanadi. He gently lifted the coiled snake up with the broadside of his machete so we could all get a good look at him without getting too close and personal. After all, this small snake is responsible for more deaths in South and Central America than all other species put together. Once our curiosity was satisfied, the guide turned the reptile loose and it slithered off into the underbrush.

We resumed our trek along the trail that took us through creeks, around fallen logs and over small rises. The beauty of the jungle with its diverse foliage kept me constantly in a state of awe. Added to this was the melody coming from the different birds and insects surrounding us.

"Venga," motioned the guide, as he paused by a hole in the earth. "Mira."

He took a long piece of grass, put it in the hole, and wiggled it around. Soon, out crawled a tarantula, following this piece of grass just like a cat chasing a piece of string. The guide then brought his hand up behind the huge spider and placed his middle finger in the centre of its thorax. He hooked the hind two legs with his thumb and small finger, and then lifted it up to give us all a closer look.

Class was now in session.

"The fangs that you see here are how he injects his poison into his prey," he explained. "It isn't that bad, really. What can be worse is the powder that he has all over his fur. If I were to let go of these legs right now, he would started scratching himself like a dog and the powder would be spread all over me. It's nearly impossible to get off, and causes severe itching."

After describing the odd behaviours of the little beast, he then placed the spider on the T-shirt of his protesting partner.

"No, I don't want him on me, get him off," yelled the alarmed guide.

We all stood about laughing at the afflicted guide's discomfort as he attempted to rid himself of this unwelcome guest. Just as we'd been told, the tarantula quickly responded by scratching his furry back, emitting a cloud of powder that floated down and settled on the poor fellows legs. The first guide then removed the furry creature from the shirt of his assistant, who then ran quickly to a nearby creek to wash off. That didn't seem to help much, and for the rest of the day, there was some heavy scratching going on.

Little did we know that the tarantula would turn out to be our appetizer that evening! We arrived at our destination and once more, I was awe-stricken. In the center of the enchanted forest was a crystal-clear pool. Suspended from a branch was a vine ideal for swinging out and splashing down in the refreshing water. The laguna was fed by a set of rapids that flowed over a smooth rock formation, creating a natural water slide. Hence the name, Tobagan. . While we frolicked in this jungle amusement park, the guides set up camp and prepared supper.

Tired from the hike and water sports, we soon gathered about the fire – hungry and tired. But the day's adventures weren't over yet. Our host appeared with our appetizer – tarantula shish kabob. He knelt and placed the skewered spider over the fire.

"Anyone hungry?" he asked. "It's quite good, but we don't eat the lethal parts."

"Are you kidding?" responded one of the gang.

"Not me," said another.

"I want some," I said, never one to miss an extraordinary experience.

Our furry friend was soon roasted and I was handed one of his cooked legs. Although shy on content, the taste was exquisite, somewhat like crabmeat, and I was left craving for more. Alas, there was a limited supply, so I had to settle for the main course, which was yucca, fish, and beans. Cooked over the fire, it was a meal divine. It wasn't long before my hammock beckoned me, and despite the numerous snake stories told around the campfire, I slept like a log.

After breakfast and a short swim the following morning, we hiked back out to the river, and returned downstream in the bongo to Puerto Ayacucho. Our excursion over, I was listless and yearning for more thrills. Damian (a young fellow from Switzerland), and I set out to find someone willing to take us white water rafting on the infamous rapids of the Orinoco at Puerto Ayacucho. We found a small company that had a large Zodiak raft with a forty horsepower motor. The owner/operator was European, spoke English and was a lively character.

"We want to go rafting on the river," I informed the owner.

"I need three customers to make ends meet," he responded.

"What if we pay for the third person?" asked Damian.

"Well, that would be less weight, and a wilder ride," the guide replied laughing.

"That's exactly what we're looking for," I said. "Forget we're tourists, and imagine you're out there alone. I get a feeling you'd just love to get out there and let her rip. Now's your chance."

"Sign this waiver, but remember, you asked for it!" he said, with a devilish look in his eye.

When will I ever learn to be careful what I ask for! The guide took us for two very wild rides down the rapids, which left us begging for more. Up we went a third time. Now the guide pulled out all the tricks in his basket, and hit the waves with a newfound ferocity. With forty horses pushing us, we crashed into a wave so huge, the raft buckled. A blanket of water smashed into me and I literally tore one hand-strap off the Zodiak. Damian and the guide thought I went over the side. So did I. But, amazingly, I was still in the raft and so were they. Beaten into submission, I said 'Uncle' and we concluded our rafting experience with that immense adrenalin rush.

This set of white water had a grim history – and I knew it –, but with today's modern watercraft, the peril had been somewhat minimized. That still did not take away from the thrill and we both agreed we had received much more than our moneys worth on that ride. Later, as we stood on the riverbank congratulating ourselves on our accomplishment, a native came gracefully flowing down through the cascades in his dugout canoe! Effortlessly, he negotiated the rushing waters, and paused in an eddy to do some fishing. So much for expecting any hero worship for our feat.

After a good sleep in a local hotel, I returned to the tour company to see if they had another voyage into the jungle that I could embark on. It turned out they did, but there was a catch: it would not be a tour per se. The company had permission to go into a new territory where the natives had not felt the incursion of tourists so far. If I wanted to join them, I was welcome to tag along, but I wouldn't be catered too. Four British medical students also requested to be part of the expedition and we five foreigners agreed to provide for ourselves, cook and assist setting up camp. Little did I know, but I was about to embark on the most breathtaking excursion I had ever experienced. I was about to see the jungle in 3-D; enhanced with smells and sounds!

We set forth the following day in our thatch-roofed bongo, headed up the Orinoco again. After a few hours on this large river, we headed up a smaller river named Sipapo. This was a much more laid-back trip than the previous one, and the guides were just as excited as we were. Travelling into the unknown creates a unique kind of camaraderie.

After some time, the pilot of the boat slowed down and turned up a barely visible little tributary. Idling our way up this narrow stream, the jungle crowded in on us from both sides. There were lonely orchids shouting out their brilliant red amidst a sea of green.

The tree trunks were wearing their camouflage colours, like hunters infiltrating the forest. From a lighter shade of pale to a starker hue of green, it was all distinguishable. Now this was what I had been searching for! We wound our way upstream for about an hour, with each bend unmasking new splendour. Suddenly, the sky burst open above us as we floated out onto a small lake. The scene was idyllic! A huge tepui loomed up over the jungle horizon and reflected on the mirror-like surface of the lagoon. I spotted a native settlement nestled on the far shore.

"Look – over there –," I exclaimed, pointing at the village.

"That is where we hope to spend the night," said one of our guides. "Pepe and I are going to walk into the village to meet with the people. We hope they welcome us, but you never know. The rest of you wait here in the boat until we get back."

The worried tone of the guide's voice, and expression on his face, brought me around to reality. No, this was not a typical tour. The natives here were not used to intruders, and we were not sure what kind of reception lay in store. Arrows or food, what would it be?

It wasn't long before the guides returned saying that they had received a warm welcome. We gathered up our belongings and walked into the village. The smiling, but quiet, villagers stared at us curiously, as we filed into their community. This was an extraordinary event for them, akin to aliens landing. As for myself, I was just relieved to see their smiles.

We got ourselves settled in, and then proceeded to acquaint ourselves with our gracious hosts. As usual, the children came forward first. A young boy about five years old quickly became our guide, friend and source of amusement for the days to follow. One of the med students gave him a harmonica; therefore, we could always tell where the young lad was. The elders only spoke Piaroa, their native language. As they slowly warmed to our presence, we had some very interesting conversations. Our one guide who spoke Piaroa, interpreted what the natives said into Spanish; I in turn, translated it into English for the rest of the crew. And vice versa.

I soon observed that after dark was time for personal hygiene, as families one by one went down to the lake to bathe. This amazed me, as they had no flashlights, and of course, I had visions of all the electric eels, stingrays and piranha lurking in the dark waters. After all, I had seen members of the village catching piranha in this same spot earlier.

The next day I spent mainly with the young boy who showed me around while the tour operators visited and negotiated with the villagers. Up little trails we went, his young hand pointing to this plant and that, saying good to eat, not good to eat or don't touch. We encountered many different species of insects and small animals that I had never seen in magazines or on TV.

My young friend suddenly stopped and pointed at a funny little creature sitting on a very big leaf.

"Don't touch little caterpillar," he said in his broken, child-like Spanish. "See spikes on his back? They will poke your skin and make you sick. Look, he has a hard coat like an armadillo." (I later learned that this was a Saddle Back Caterpillar.)

My next lesson was how to catch a real armadillo. I found myself being stared at by a small armoured creature nearly obscured by the underbrush. I rushed forward, trying to catch him, but he ran faster than I could have ever imagined.

"No, no. You have to walk slow. From front. He can't see you when you're in front. No supper tonight" said my little friend, giggling.

I also observed numerous fruit bats hanging from the branches of trees surrounding the miniature lake. It seemed that everywhere I looked, there was some form of plant or animal life that was foreign to my eyes.

On the third day of our stay with these hospitable people, it was decided that the whole crew would head further up the Sipapo River to talk with other tribes. One of the English gents and I elected to stay behind to do some exploring on our own. With a couple of very small dugout canoes, we set off to explore the small stream feeding the lake, and... maybe even encounter an anaconda. These small boats did not allow for a lot of movement; in fact, if I sat at the wrong end, it just sank. We had not progressed very far up the stream when we encountered a fallen tree that we needed to duck under. I had just negotiated this manoeuvre when my friend yelled,

"Ron, look out! There's a water snake coming up behind you."

I swivelled to see a huge, multi-coloured snake swimming toward me, just below the water's surface. The clear water was only about a meter deep at this point, which made it was easy to see all his distinctive features. The first shock was that he had the true colours of a South American coral snake. Contrary to the North American ones, here I had been taught 'red on black, don't look back, red on yellow, friendly fellow'. This snake's colours said 'don't look back'! The only problem with this conclusion was that my knowledge of corals had them about baby finger size, and only inches long. This snake was a meter long and at least four centimetres in diameter! The second startling factor was that he was swimming in the water like a fish; not skimming the surface, as I'd observed other snakes do.

The formidable foe approached my canoe and hesitated, as if deciding whether to go over or under this ungainly 'log.' Poised with my paddle ready for combat, my heart was racing and fear coursed through my veins. I was afraid that if I moved too much, water would pour over the side of the canoe and I would be at the snake's mercy. Those snake-eyes didn't appear too merciful! Fortunately, the boat stayed afloat, and the large serpent decided to go under my canoe. He rose up out of the water and slithered along a tree stump. After a short pause, he returned to the water directly in front of me. Then he did something I would not have believed if I hadn't seen it with my own eyes. He coiled up on the bottom of the stream as if ready to strike, and sat motionless. Now I could plainly see the rings of colour going right around his body, so any doubt about this being a real coral were erased. Red, black and yellow, this was a dangerous fellow. After a moment or two, he raised his head above water, took in some air, and returned to his original position, head poised for action. My fear had somewhat abated and I became absolutely fascinated with his behaviour. It was as if he was guarding his territory and telling us this was as far as we go. When he started to uncoil and come back in my direction, I agreed with him.

"Back up, back up, let's get outa here," I shouted at my partner. We back paddled, ducking under the fallen tree, and departed that creek as fast as our little boats would permit.

"Did you see what I saw?" I asked my friend.

"I think so, but it's hard to believe. Was that a real coral?"

"It had the right colours and they went all around his body. But the course I took in Maturin on snakes never mentioned anything about a coral that size!"

We arrived back at the settlement about the same time as the others did, and we were all clamouring to be heard; it turned out that they had some adversity of their own. When we shared our snaky encounter first, they laughed, suggesting that our story wasn't unlike the big fish that got away.

Their source of excitement happened upstream where hostile natives threw rocks and sticks at them. The message had been quite clear, "WE DON'T WANT YOU HERE!"

Therefore, even though our present hosts had been quite hospitable, the surrounding residents were giving us a different message – no outsiders wanted! This caused me to rethink my whole tourism idea. I decided it was best to leave these people alone so they could continue to live their enviable lifestyle; simple, natural and at one with the elements.

Later in the evening, while sitting around the campfire, I shared our snake experience with the elder. He chuckled and said in his language,

"That was Rolla, that is his place you visited. He is a "water coral" and very, very deadly. You are lucky he let you out of there. He has been there for years."

Oh, the smell of redemption can be sweet at times!

Somehow, during the course of our stay in the village, I had gained the hearts of these sincere and simple people. A couple of the men tried very hard to talk me into coming to live with them, permanently. This was a real honour and I desperately wanted to accept their invitation. They described how they would all pull together to build me a house, show me their ways, and even find me a suitable companion. When I mentioned this to the guides, they said they couldn't leave me there, as they would be in trouble with the authorities. Oh yes, the real world. I don't like to say I have regrets, but I often feel haunted by this lost opportunity.

Sadly, on the fourth day, we had to leave the friendly Piaroa and their paradise. We floated downstream towards civilization, but we weren't out of the woods yet. On the way, we encountered a small water coral acting just as we had described. How do you not say, 'I told you so?' We saw numerous other types of snakes, but the one that impressed us most was very large black serpent sunning himself on a log.

To put a finishing touch on this extreme adventure, we floated down the Sipapo River in our life jackets and had the thrill of seeing a stingray shoot out from the sand beneath us.

Now, with some misgivings, I was ready to return to the 'outside world'. My dream of a jungle tourist camp had just been dashed, and I had forfeited a once in a lifetime chance to live the simple life. Now my life was about to get seriously complicated. As well, a very bizarre epilogue to this most recent adventure was to be added by my mother during my next phone call home.

Chapter 18

M Y ARRIVAL BACK into the noisy city of Caracas required my reluctant release of where I had just been, and for acceptance of where I now was. Car horns replaced the sound of Macaws, the serene flow of the river now a metal stream of moving cars, and concrete and asphalt took the place of green foliage and fertile soil. Yes, civilization and all its amenities were once more at my disposal.

"Mexico? Are you serious?"

"Yes," said Brent, "we need you to go to Mexico City, rent an office or apartment and hire an administrator. We have an older lady there now, but I'm afraid this seismic world is a little much for her. Looks like we have landed a big contract over there and already have a crew in country drilling."

"When do I have to go? My son is supposed to be coming down for his summer holidays in July."

"After you set things up in Mexico City, you can go out to the job site over by the Gulf, hire and train a field administrator, and then head back here. Shouldn't take too long, probably a couple of months."

Never a dull moment in this industry, as I now readied myself for this new challenge. I called my parents to let them know of this new development and to share my most recent experiences.

"What in the heck were you up to two weeks ago?" my mother demanded.

"Why, what are you talking about?" was my immediate and somewhat shocked reaction.

"Every time you were in trouble in the old days I used to get an awful premonition, and I haven't felt that since 1981, when you changed your life around. Two weeks ago, I had that feeling again. I sensed it was unrelated to drugs or alcohol, but I knew you were in some kind of trouble."

"Well, Mom, I had a little run in with a snake that scared the hell out of me about that time. I guess you felt my fear. Obviously five-thousand miles doesn't make much difference when dealing with a mother's intuition, does it?" I said laughing. Further discussion revealed that she had this feeling at the exact time of my encounter with the water coral snake. A mother's sixth sense truly knows no bounds.

My exit from the airport terminal in Mexico City was pandemonic to say the least. Joining a long line up of people waiting for taxis, I soon discovered that they crammed as many individuals into these small VW taxis as they could, sorting the fares by destination. With the passenger seat removed, these were very cramped quarters indeed. I did not want to share a cab, so after a lot of haggling, I got my way and rode away solitaire.

When the taxi pulled up in front of the luxurious El Presidenté Hotel, I realized that my stay here was not going to be hard to take. Upon settling in, I discovered that I had come through customs with my hashish looking yopo. I would have had a hard time explaining that one to the Federales! I wasted no time in ridding myself of this 'gift from the Shaman' to avoid making the same mistake again.

"Welcome to Mexico!" exclaimed Pat, the country manager. It turned out that he was from the same part of Canada as me; we quickly became friends. The first and most difficult task was going to be dealing with our interim secretary, Señora Rosa. I needed her aid in accomplishing what we had to do, but what she would be doing was ultimately eliminating her job. This was a delicate situation to say the least.

Early the following morning, Señora Rosa and I met in our makeshift office at the hotel and I sadly realized this was going to be even more difficult than I imagined. She was a pleasant, senior lady, very cultured and spoke good English. The rough language and mannerisms of the oil industry had already become difficult for her to contend with. Nevertheless, when I told her that we would have to hire someone more versatile, she broke down in tears.

"This job is going to require a lot of working with numbers, minor accounting and trips to the various projects. It will require staying in rustic camps for several days at a time," I explained, trying to console her with the facts.

This had a positive effect and slowly her mood shifted. So much so, that she helped me rent an apartment, run an ad in the paper and ultimately hire a young male administrator. Within a couple of weeks, I was able to leave Mexico City with things in fine order. I flew over to Tampico and drove two hours out to our field operations. Once on site, I hired and trained a young fellow to become the administrator there. That too went quite well, and in no time, my services in Mexico were no longer required.

Back in Venezuela, I now awaited the arrival of my fifteen-year-old son, who was flying solo from Calgary to Caracas. With plane changes required in Dallas and Miami, I was one anxious parent. With a small monetary "donation," I was able to pass through security and meet Shaine as he got off the plane. That way, I could assist him getting through the language barrier at customs. All went well and soon he was accompanying me out of the terminal. What a feat, at his age, to have the courage to tackle such a journey, with plane connections to make in strange cities, and ending up in a country with a foreign language.

His entry into my new world was an exciting time for both of us, and I wasted no time introducing Shaine to the wonders of Latin America. Caracas, as was expected, was a real culture shock for him. Coming from a relatively small city east of Calgary, this city of six million plus people was just a bit overwhelming for my son. Therefore, it was off to the seashore on Margarita Island to stay with Dick's family, who had just recently moved down from my hometown. With someone close to his own age to chum around with, Shaine and Michael were soon good buddies. With so much to do, and so little time (as he was to be with me for only one month), we left our friends for a week, to travel down to Angel Falls. This turned out to be the most memorable trip one could ever ask for, in more ways than one.

With a rented truck we proceeded south, across the ferry and down to my favourite haunt, Pto. Ordaz. I arranged a tour through the local airline (Avensa), boarded a DC- 3 and flew into the land of tepuys. It was truly like something out of a '1950's movie, the old plane flying low and between these flat top plateaus. Below lay virgin jungle, with waterways carving up the landscape. The only access to this area was by plane or water. Landing in Canaima, the guide told us we would not be setting out for a while, so to relax and enjoy the scenery. It did not take long to take in all the sights and have a bite besides. We sat back at the airstrip, patiently waiting to get started on our trek, and observed others returning from their expedition to the falls. I could not see one happy face in the bunch. Grumbling, complaining, yelling and other forms of human discontent abounded. I had to find out what was going on, so I approached one of the disgruntled.

"What is everyone so upset about?"

"These fools ran out of water and food. The boats were overloaded and they didn't even have enough life jackets to go around. It was just a mad dash up and back, so we sure didn't get to experience much. We're just glad to be back safe and sound and sure won't do that again."

I approached another person coming in off a different tour, and he had the same story. Two hours passed, our guide had not returned and now I was getting apprehensive. I watched another unhappy tourist cursing one of the tour operators, and once more heard the dismal tale.

"Shaine," I said, "I don't like the looks of this. Yes, I would like to see Angel Falls, but not that badly. Listen to these people. They sound like they have been to hell and back. How 'bout we say to heck with this and catch the next plane out of here?"

"It's up to you Dad."

Wandering over to the kiosk that housed our travel company, I told the tour promoter I wanted our money back and would like to catch the next plane back to Pto. Odaz. When I explained why, he suggested we contact some women who owned a resort above the falls at Canaima. He claimed they had their own tours to Angel Falls, and if I wanted, he would see if they had room for us. Even better, he said he would transfer our tour money to them if this could be arranged.

My Higher Power must have felt that we deserved a break, since He stepped in with another miracle. What started out looking like a disaster suddenly became a holiday not even I could have concocted. The three German ladies did find a way to slip us into their camp. Established by their father (Jungle Rudy) in the early 50's, it was the first such camp in the area and the only one to have an auxiliary camp at the base of the main attraction, Angel Falls. We rode to the top of the panoramic set of falls we had viewed from Canaima, in a cart pulled by a farm tractor. Once there, we shuffled into a boat and headed upriver to Camp Ucaima.

We arrived at the camp shortly and were amazed to see a nicely groomed site, complete with European style cabins. Clean and neat, the whole site radiated the female touch. There was even indoor plumbing! Now this was more like it. Service, both pleasant and accommodating, was a very welcome attraction after viewing the trauma experienced below.

Once settled in, we had a chance to check out the surroundings. Animals of all sorts abounded; ducks, iguanas, monkeys, sloths, peacocks, parrots and macaws graced the grounds. Since this was a small camp, the setting was serene and quiet. This was one of the most welcome parts of the whole experience. Peace, quiet and tranquility slowly began to permeate my soul.

Meals were a communal affair, and it was here that we met our fellow guests. An adventurous lot they were, with ages ranging from a couple of twelve-year-old boys to an Italian couple in their sixties.

There were sixteen guests including ourselves. It was decided that we would travel upriver to Angel Falls two days hence, which left us the following day to explore other areas.

After breakfast, we set out for Salto Sapo (Frog Falls). With a forty horsepower motor powering our launch, we soon arrived at the top of these thunderous falls. Trepidation overtook me as I realized the danger we were in. We headed into shore, with the foaming precipice looming much too closely.

"Shaine, if that motor stops, jump in and swim like crazy!"

"I'm not a very good swimmer," he replied, with a look of fear in his eyes.

(Six months after our exploit, a boat with twenty-one European tourists had the motor stall on their boat at a similar falls. Where this disaster occurred, someone had had the foresight to suspend a cable across the river just above the roaring falls. Seven people managed to grab hold of the cable; sadly, the other fourteen plunged to their deaths.)

There was no such cable at these falls. There were some tense moments as we approached the shore only three-hundred meters from certain death. Once safely on shore, our guide led us down a path that suddenly disappeared into the backside of the frothing falls. . The next moments seemed like an eternity as we clung to a narrow ledge, while grasping a rope and inching our way forward through the blinding spray. The deafening roar, back spray and wind all pushed my nerves to the limit. Most of the time visibility was nonexistent, so we made our way forward with our eyes closed, holding on desperately to the rope. With great relief, we finally exited the ominous cavern into the glorious sunshine.

"Indian Jones has nothing on us!" I hollered above the roar of the falls.

"Wow!" exclaimed Shaine. "That was awesome."

Admittedly, there now was a bit of apprehension about having to re-enter that formidable cave. Had there been an alternate route, I would have taken it. But there wasn't, so into the cauldron we ventured once more. We emerged safe and sound on the other side with an unforgettable thrill firmly embedded into our memory.

We proceeded to the bottom of the falls, where we swam off the remaining tension and gloried in our accomplishment. Once mellowed out, we hiked back up the trail to our boat. We then ventured out to an island positioned at the top of the waterfalls. Some of the more daring members of our crew decided to cross over to another small island, wading through shallow but fast moving water just above the falls.

"C'mon Dad, lets go over there."

"No, Shaine, enough already. One slip and you're gone! You'd be over the falls in a heartbeat," I said, pointing at the water disappearing over the edge in a flurry of mist.

When the others returned from their exploits, we called it a day and returned to camp. We had a quick meal and then it was siesta time. Once rested, Shaine and I asked for the services of a guide to take us into a native village. This required motoring up a tributary of the main river to where we found the trailhead to the village. After a twenty-minute walk through dense jungle, we broke into a clearing filled with small clay huts. The villagers welcomed us warmly, despite our unannounced visit. They didn't get many visitors into their village, so they delighted in showing us some of their ways. It was here that I learned about the yucca plant and how it was processed into manioc. Their simple and gracious manner of living seemed to magnify the complexity of my own life. We concluded our very pleasant visit with the natives and returned downstream to our materialistic paradise.

The next morning I arose filled with excitement. We were going to travel by boat up the turbulent Rio Carrao to the base of Angel Falls.

Our trip began in a relaxing fashion. We stopped at a small village where Shaine bought a blowgun and darts. Farther on, we found ourselves dashing out from behind a waterfall into a placid pool of water. The trip up the river proved to be an adventure in itself, with numerous rapids to mount and spectacular views to behold. As we rounded one corner, I counted ten very high water falls cascading off the tops of the surrounding tepuys. Finally, towards the end of the day, we rounded a bend, and suddenly, there it was; Angel Falls, the highest waterfall in the world!

"Now I see why people go to such lengths to see those falls," I said, almost in a whisper.

"When I saw all the other ones, I didn't expect this one to be any different. This is beyond amazing," Shaine responded.

We arrived at our stone hut camp and were busy snapping pictures while the guides prepared supper. Early in the morning, the falls were clearly visible, as clouds had not yet moved in. By the time breakfast was complete and we started our trek up to the base of the falls, clouds had completely obscured the top of the tepuy.

"Shaine, check this out." I had stopped to observe an unusual looking spider in his web.

"No," he said, with a slight smirk.

"C'mon, don't be scared of it."

"No," laughed Shaine.

Suddenly my feet began to burn; I looked down and quickly realized I was standing on an anthill, with hundreds of the little hellions commencing to bite the foot that was now feeding them. This was why Shaine was laughing. I jumped and frantically proceeded to rid my feet of these devilish critters, while my son kept a safe distance and enjoyed my antics.

Finally rid of the ants, we resumed our gruelling one-hour hike up to the base of Angel Falls. My exhaustion was quickly forgotten as the spectacle unfolded before me. I stood for a time silently marvelling at this wondrous work of nature. Peering upward, all I could see was water falling from the clouds, the top of the tepuy obscured. My eyes followed the the silver stream downward. After a free-fall of nine-hundred and seventy-nine metres, it briefly touched a rocky ledge and was airborne once more. After the water had plummeted a total of thirteen hundred metres, it finally came to rest in a swirling pool. The scene was beyond words.

After about two hours of exciting repose, we made our way back down the path to the river. Back in the boat, we charged downstream, this time flying down the rapids instead of struggling up them. Our trip back to our main camp was far quicker than the one upstream had been.

We spent the final day of our stay floating down a small river in plastic kayaks. A young Venezuelan lad, about twelve-years old, had no family with him and was overjoyed when Shaine and I invited him along. We had the guide take us upriver in the big boat and drop us off with the kayaks. We spent the whole day swimming, kayaking and exploring, just the three of us. What a climax to a wondrous journey, one we would forever cherish.

We returned to the beaches of Margarita and spent the rest of Shaine's vacation splashing in salt water. Time flew quickly and soon Shaine boarded a plane and returned home, his head filled with some extraordinary tales to share with his classmates. I returned to my job and its own peculiar and adventuresome twists. Life also had a huge shocker waiting for me, one that would forever alter my world.

Chapter 19

'RON, YOUR DAUGHTER Julie phoned and wants you to call her.' I slowly digested the content of the note on the kitchen table. I had arrived home late to our apartment in Caracas and now found myself in utter shock. Every emotion possible overwhelmed me, as I grasped the reality of what these few words meant.

Back in 1975, Julie had been a sweet, little, five-year old who adored her rambling father. Then suddenly I disappeared, with no explanation. No more visits, letters or phone calls. It was now 1994, and my regret for that immature and reckless decision had been haunting me for years. My daughter would be about twenty-four years old now. What would she be feeling? Resentment? Anger? Indifference?

I knew what I felt. Fear, shame and guilt. Nevertheless, I had also looked forward to this day. I'd searched all over for her during the '80's, but could not locate her. This important amend had persistently vexed me. Waves of love and happiness flooded away my apprehension. I slowly made my way to the telephone. I dialled the number written on the note.

With every ring of the phone, I fought back urges to quickly hang up. One part of me was hoping that no one would answer, while another was full of anticipation. After what seemed an eternity, the ringing ceased. A voice on the other end of the line said,

"Hello."

"Julie?"

"Yes, who's this?"

"You're Dad, Julie…it's your Dad," I said quietly, as I fought back the tears welling up inside.

Exclamations of joy and delight flowed through the phone line.

"I am so sorry Julie, I don't even………."

"Dad, all I want is to have you back in my life," she said, cutting me off. "I'm just so glad I've finally found you."

"And so am I! But how did you ever do that, with me way down here?"

"I ran an ad looking for my father in the newspaper of your hometown. Your step-daughter seen it and told your brother. He gave me your number."

"Well, both of them knew I was looking for you. In fact, Jackie was with me once when I went searching for you. I'm so glad she seen it. But it must have taken a lot of courage for you to put an ad like that in the paper."

"I've wanted to do it for a long time. I can't believe I'm finally talking to you!"

We talked for a long time, and I found out that not only did I have a daughter again, but also two grandsons and a granddaughter as well. Julie was married and living about an hour away from my hometown.

I had not planned to return to Canada for Christmas that year, but how could I not go home now? After all, I had just received the most fantastic Christmas surprise one could ever ask for. This was one gift that was meant to be shared, experienced and savoured.

As it was the beginning of December, all flights leaving the country were overbooked for the whole month of December. No air transport of any kind, direct or otherwise, was available. I had only one choice and that was to return to the Venezuelan way of doing things.

At three in the morning, I went to the airport and bought a plane ticket, which I hoped would get me placed on standby. With Yvette along to assist in the process, we paid off the agent in charge of boarding passes and I started to play the waiting game.

Unfortunately, that morning the agent's boss was watching far too closely for him to allow me through customs. He did, however, assure me that he would get me past customs the next morning, just no guarantee that I would get on the plane. The following morning found me hounding this same agent once more. During a quiet time, he gave me a boarding pass and I slipped through customs into the waiting area. One of the flight attendants asked me for my boarding pass, and when she seen I was on stand-by, she laughed and said,

"You haven't got a chance, honey. This flight is overbooked by at least ten passengers, so we will be paying people just to give up their seats."

Dejected, I sat, waited and prayed. I felt certain that my goal was in God's plan, so I had to have faith He would help me attain it. The plane started boarding, and just as the stewardess had said, people were now leaving the plane and giving up their seats for cash. What a feeling of futility as I stood and watched a flood of people disembark the plane.

Finally, when the last person was off, the flight attendant turned to me and said,

"I'm so sorry. I really do hope you can catch a plane tomorrow." So, that was that! I watched her proceed down the gangway to the plane.

All that could alter the course of events now would be a pure and unadulterated miracle.

"Janet," yelled a flight attendant from the plane, "I made a mistake and paid off one too many people, so if you have anyone left out there, we have one seat." How can one not believe in the power of prayer with miracles like this!

"C'mon," said Janet, turning to me standing back at the entrance, "Let's go."

As I sat on that plane, saying a prayer of thanks, I could not help but wonder why God was so gracious with me. Although a drifter most of my life, God still chose to work wonders for me, despite my erring ways. I could only surmise that when I was following His will, He confirmed His appreciation under the guise of coincidence.

After all the years of wondering and worrying about what it would be like meeting Julie again, there was indeed some trepidation. However, I was welcomed with open arms, not only by Julie, her husband and my three grandchildren, but also by her grandparents who had every reason to harbour severe resentments towards me. Julie's mother was also there and surprised me by bearing no ill feelings. Guilt soon dissipated with such honest and pardoning acceptance of my shortcomings. They accepted my sincere apologies and now it was up to me to follow that up by active reconciliation. I could learn so much from these benevolent souls.

After a beautiful holiday with my new family, I returned to visit with my folks. These bountiful blessings in my life had begun to materialize when I adopted a program of living that included dependence upon a Higher Power. So, I attended some all-important meetings to fortify myself for the periods ahead when such support would be absent. Then it was back to warmer climes once more.

Upon arriving back in Venezuela, I discovered that Yvette had not expounded on any of the opportunities we had worked on so diligently. We had connected with the biggest tour operator on Margarita Island and all that was required was to send him some tourists. My job with Destiny was taking up most of my time now, so the tourism factor was up to Yvette. For whatever reason, she was unable to acquire even one client for them. Then, to add insult to injury, she disappeared with my cell phone for a few days, ringing up a substantial bill. Thus, that relationship came to an abrupt end!

Destiny had projects going on all over the country and they were constantly trying to make their operations more cost effective. This was a monumental task, with the radical labour situation a constant variable. The focus turned to innovative methods of seismic drilling, which was an exciting time for everyone, but also costly for the company. It seemed for every positive step forward, there were an equal number of setbacks. Throughout this period, as the company's future in this foreign land became more uncertain, I became increasingly convinced I wanted to remain in Venezuela. I decided to take a break and assess my options.

At Easter, I flew home, rented a car and took Shaine to West Yellowstone for four wondrous days of snowmobiling. This splendid holiday also provided an opportunity to assess my alternatives in South America. I realized I had to commit myself somehow, so I purchased five-hundred brilliantly coloured bandanas in El Paso to begin a new venture in Venezuela. I was certain these headpieces would sell like hotcakes in a land where free enterprise flourished. Back in Caracas, I started a small expediting company, taking on a partner named Darren. His father, Bill, was an American expat, who could be found any evening at the chess tables in Plaza Venezuela. Bill was a very trustworthy soul. He kept me posted on current events within the country and always seemed to know what was going on in the distant mining fields. Darren had inherited his father's amiable qualities.

I now had a cedula making me a permanent resident, which allowed us to form a limited company without any problem. We rented an apartment that became the office of Inversiones Daron and served as our living quarters. Arrangements were made with a broker to import and export all sorts of items in and out of the country expeditiously. While in Canada, I had also formed an association with an oilfield supply company. On my flights to Miami, I arranged with some major companies to distribute their products in Venezuela. The future looked bright, with lots of possibilities.

I attempted to start unloading the bandanas by finding street vendors interested in peddling them. As these bands of cloth did not come with an instruction manual, the Caraqueños did not seem to grasp their value. Not to be discouraged, I presented them on the beaches of Margarita, where they once more failed to garner the interest I had hoped for. Frustration started to set in. To make matters worse, when I sent a shipment of alpaca and llama knit sweaters north, the Guardia pilfered some, and my profit completely vanished. Needless to say, that curtailed further shipments through that corrupt channel.

So, while I struggled to get my new company off the ground, Destiny was having its own problems. Despite manufacturing efficient drilling equipment, the radical labour situation constantly hampered profitable production. It appeared to be just a matter of time before they would cut their losses and leave Venezuela.

One day, while I sat pondering my future at my favourite hang-out, the Gran Café, I spotted a Caucasian fellow sitting alone.

"Hi, mind if I join you?" I asked, introducing myself.

"Sure, have a seat. My name is Jergen."

"So, what brings you to this part of the world?"

"I live on a sailboat. I'm from Norway, but live out in the Caribbean. I'm in town to pick up supplies, and get a new Zodiak. Mine was stolen."

"Well, maybe I can help you with that," I said.

We set out to find a distributor for these rubber rafts, and it wasn't long before we found a supplier and got a price. Jergen lived on a very strict budget, so he deferred making this major purchase, on the faint hope that maybe the police had recovered his lost craft.

"How would you like to sail with us to Bon Aire?" Jergen asked.

"Who's 'us'?"

"I met a Venezuelan lady about six months ago, and she's been living and sailing about with me ever since," Jergen replied.

"Well, I have a bunch of bandanas I'm trying to unload, so maybe I could get rid of them over there."

"There are a couple of catches though. We probably won't sail for a couple of weeks, and for you to come along, which would be great, I still have to get an okay from my partner," Jergen said, a slight smile curling from his lips.

"Well, why don't you bring her up for supper tonight at our place?"

Thus, the stage was set. The two sailors arrived that evening, and I was introduced to Alvira. She and I hit it off right away, and in the course of the evening, she invited me to join them on the trip to Bon Aire. When she turned to ask Jergen if that would be okay by him, I struggled hard to keep a straight face.

Two days later, the three of us arrived in Pto. Cabello by bus and made our way to the dock. Their forty foot sloop, a beautiful, sleek, sailing craft, lay anchored in the calm harbour not far from shore. A bit of good fortune came Jergen's way, as the police had recovered his Zodiak. So, instead of hiring a boat to transport us back and forth to their home on water, we were able to commence provisioning right away with the reclaimed rubber raft. I soon learned that a sailor's life is not a laid-back one. Packing groceries, cleaning, scraping barnacles, painting and applying weather resistant coatings were just a few of the tasks I found myself doing. More than once it crossed my mind that maybe I had just been invited along as a source of cheap labour.

Finally, we set sail. I was surprised at how quickly I fell into rhythm with the waves and soon discovered I could even read a book without becoming nauseated. The same could not be said for Alvira. She spent all fifteen hours of the crossing below deck.

We arrived in the port of Kralendijk, Bon Aire, very late at night. I took over the helm, while Jergen leaned over the bow and shouted instructions; guiding us safely through the maze of fishing boats anchored in the darkness. We found a safe place to nestle between them and set anchor. Tired, I said a quick 'Good Night', crawled into my hammock on the upper deck and was soon fast asleep.

"Ron, HELP!" came a cry from down below.

I ran down the steps into the hold and found Alvira on top of Jergen, with a knife in her hand, trying to stab him. He had a hold of her arm, but his situation was very precarious. Instinctively, I grabbed the knife from Alvira's hand and pulled her off Jergen. Once free, he took control of the situation, and set about calming her down. I didn't have a clue what this was all about, nor did I want any part of it. I returned up top with the knife, and spent the rest of the night lying in my hammock with one eye open.

In the morning, on the pretext of registering the boat in the country, we set forth in the Zodiak, leaving Alvira on the boat. On the way to shore, Jergen said,

"She gets crazy sometimes. This isn't the first time. I have to get rid of her or she's going to be the death of me. She has some mental disorder, I think. There is no rhyme or reason for these attacks."

Jergen paused, and then asked, "How would you like to sail around the world with me?"

"Certainly not with her on board," I declared.

He laughed, "No, it's time for her to go. I'm going to see if I can get her sent back to Venezuela, and get help removing her from the boat."

"Well, I have my stuff with me. I'm not returning to the boat if she's still there. I'm going to try to sell these bandanas while you get her on her way. Then, yes, I think this might just be the adventure I've been looking for."

We proceeded to customs where the officers informed us that they would help with the extraction, but not until the following day. Therefore, I informed Jergen that I was going to stay at a Naturist Resort that happened to be on the island, and to come and get me when all was in order.

I soon had sixty bandanas sold, so I headed for the resort with some extra cash in my pocket. And what a beautiful place; quiet, serene, and most important, no trauma. The freedom experienced when clothes are shed is exhilarating and I quickly adapted to the nudist lifestyle.

Jergen never did come for me, and so I missed out on what seemed like another golden opportunity. In retrospect, this was probably another example of my Higher Power protecting me from myself. However, I certainly did enjoy the reprieve on the beach, and after a few days of soaking up the sun, I flew back to reality.

And reality certainly hit me with a vengeance. Destiny concluded it was time to count their losses and extract themselves from the country. They offered me a position in Ecuador, but the area they were working in was rife with rebels. I had no desire to be taken hostage and enduring what Clint had when he was held by FARC. And so I turned down the offer. I set about consolidating all the equipment in Maturin, inventorying it, and loading it into containers bound for Ecuador, Bolivia, and Miami. What remained after the containers were loaded, Destiny sold to my friends Dick and Chuck. This consisted of five trucks loaded with six quads, tools and a variety of other items. As this deal would appear to be a conflict of interest, I left the negotiation of this deal to management in Calgary.

My own company wasn't doing much better. I was premature with this venture, as the advent of the internet was yet to come. Thus, phone calls eventually out cost actual sales. Why had I not pursued Jergen on his world sailing offer or stayed to live with the Indians in the jungle? It was becoming apparent that God was not about to let me run away from the world. It seemed my drumbeat was leading me somewhere else.

Dick had been constantly pressuring me to come down to the Gran Sabana and get into diamond mining, while my old friend Albert was also urging me to check it out. According to them, it was very laid back down there, quite different from the hectic union jobs I had been working on. They were quite persuasive, and I felt myself succumbing to their pressure. But, the deciding factor came from an unexpected direction, one that would also profoundly affect my lifestyle.

One day, I noticed a lovely looking young lady standing by our field office. I casually asked the mechanic,

"Who's that?"

"That's Liz. I dated her couple of times. She's a lovely lady, but I'm leaving soon and don't want to hurt her. You're staying in country, maybe you should get to know her. She really is a super person."

It didn't take me long to introduce myself, and throughout the course of the next few days, I got to know her better. I soon realized that, as my friend had said, she was not like the other women we had met down here. Her vitality was great to be around, but I too was hesitant to get romantically involved unless I had something to offer. And right now, that wasn't much. My life was in turmoil.

Easter arrived during this hectic time, and as always, getting anything accomplished became nearly impossible. So, I decided to take a break, go south and find out what was really happening down in the Gran Sabana.

"How would you like to go to Sta Elena this Semana Santa?" I asked Liz in Spanish. "I have a bunch of bandanas I think a good salesperson could help me unload on this busy holiday week. Are you interested in making a few dollars, while at the same time getting a chance to visit the famous Parque Canaima? My friend Dick said he has a big house, with lots of room, so it won't cost you a thing."

She enthusiastically consented, and so we set out for the large southeastern portion of Venezuela known as the Gran Sabana. Once we arrived and settled in at Dick's, we quickly set up a little kiosk at the first gas station on the town's outskirts. All buses stopped there, as it was a long drive across the sabana, without any services. It took awhile, but soon we had started a fad, with university students and others liking these colourful kerchiefs. In the next few days, we sold the majority of them, and everywhere you went you could see someone sporting one of these colourful pieces of cloth.

In the course of all this, Liz and I came to know each other quite well, and a mutual feeling of affection developed. I had also decided to move to Sta. Elena for certain, as I seen many possibilities there. By the time we returned to Maturin, Liz and I had begun dating.

Once the containers were all on their way, bills paid, and the companies assets completely dispersed, I was now ready to pack up and move to Sta. Elena de Uairén. It was my turn to chase the glitter of those diamonds that had everyone bustling about. A new epic in my life was about to begin.

END of PART II

Salto Sapo

Escort from Tama Tama

Ron guiding winchline

WD Locking hubs

The Gran Sabana

Ferry across the Kukenan River

Liz meets President Caldera

The Churuata

PART III

Chapter 20

THANKS TO MY good friends Dick and Sheila, I had a place to live when I arrived in Sta. Elena de Uairén. They had recently moved there from our home town of Peace River in Northern Canada, with their two children, Loretta and Michael. Now there were five of us escapees from the chills of northern Alberta, adjusting to the life and climate of the Gran Sabana of Venezuela.

Located fifteen miles north of the Brazilian border, Sta Elena is situated on a very high and huge plateau, which provides for an idyllic climate. With a year round temperature of eighty degrees and only two seasons, wet or dry, I knew my heart had found a new home. The small town was a bustling hive of activity, due to the over-border trade with Brazil and diamond mining. Optimism radiated from every core of the community, exuded by both the locals and foreigners alike.

While in Caracas I had sold my share of the company, Inversiones Daron sa., to my partner, Darren. I then formed a new company called Drumbeats sa. With this company, my plan was to freelance myself in whatever direction destiny took me. By this time, I was a non-resident of Canada, and a full resident of Venezuela. My accountant had incorporated my company, so everything was legal and Venezuela could get its portion of my upcoming millions, or so

I dreamed. Thus prepared, I began scouting around for business. I also made a decision not to make any commitments until I had a chance to check out all my prospects.

An international convention of English speaking miners seemed to occur each morning over coffee at the local panaderia (bakery-coffee shop). It was here that I met the different players in the field of diamond mining. Americans, Canadians, Trinidadians, Europeans, Afrikaans, Guyanese, as well as English speaking Brazilians or Venezuelans gathered informally to share their present hurdles, successes and even their failures. This made for lively conversations and I accumulated a wealth of information during these sessions. One name kept coming up a lot but the person was never present – WD Allen. Referred to by the locals as Allen, and the gringos as WD, he became an enigma for me. I had met him once briefly in Caracas, but had not seen him at all since my arrival. It seemed that everyone had some comment about what WD was up to, and most seemed to hold him in high regard.

"Dick, I'd like to meet this WD character. Sounds like he has a lot of experience down here."

"No problemo, Ron, take you over to see him right now. He was working on his old truck, as usual, last time I seen him, so I'm sure we'll still find him there."

We pulled up to a large shop on the edge of town, and sure enough, there was this fellow with his head buried deep in the motor cavity of his old Toyota.

We got out of the truck and walked towards the bent over figure. Dick spoke to the invisible face, "WD... like you to meet Ron, a friend of mine from Canada."

WD lifted his head out from under the hood and turned to greet me. I faced a slender, blue-eyed man about fifty years old, 5'7" tall and sporting a grey beard. He addressed me with a heavy southern accent,

"How ya doin'? Pleased ta meet ya."

"Likewise. So, what are you up to?"

He proceeded to explain how he was having problems with the

old Toyota heating up each time he went to the mine. He had put in a new water pump but this had not rectified the problem. Now he was changing the head on the motor to see if that would resolve the situation. We soon left him to his troubles, but the door to a close friendship (that would last to this very day) had just been opened a crack.

"I'm thinking of turning part of my restaurant into a disco bar. Would you like to help me run it," Dick inquired one evening.

"As you know Dick, I came down here to get away from the noise that drives me crazy in this country. I really can't picture myself listening to that blaring music and dealing with drunks 'til the wee hours of the morning. But, I'll think on it."

In the days ahead, I assisted Dick on some projects and had the use of his old Toyota, nicknamed 'Ole Bessy'. I learned that there was a large diamond mining concession named Codza, about a five-hour drive from town (that is, when the trail was in excellent condition, which wasn't often). My friend Albert and his brother Dominique were involved in the management of it, as was Señor Tom. Tom, like myself, was from the Peace Country, but unlike me, he had been a very successful businessman. He had brought his success with him and had established himself quite well in this southern portion of the world. Soon I was doing small jobs for him and the others. WD was working on this Codza claim as well, so it was not too long before I had an opportunity to venture out to this remote area.

"So, how are you making out with the motor there WD?"

"I've changed the head. That didn't work, so now I'm changin' the whole damn motor."

"Could you use a hand?'

"Sure could. Need some parts if you wouldn't mind goin' to get 'em."

After installing the motor, WD took it for a short spin, yet the motor still heated up.

"It has to be the water pump or the rad. I put in a brand new pump, but maybe there is something wrong with it. Nothin' left to try but put in another one."

When the water pump was removed to install the newer one, the problem was discovered. The reason the motor had croaked was that a large frog had been scooped up with the water WD had gotten from a ditch. The poor creature had come to an unseemly end jammed inside. What should have been a simple remedy had cost this miner a couple of weeks of aggravation, hard work and lack of production. I could not help feeling that maybe someone unhappy with 'Allen' had chosen to cast a negative curse over him. And what could be more fitting than a frog for use in their devious scheme. It was common knowledge that many of the Brazilians in town practiced their mysterious powers of negative persuasion, commonly called 'Black Magic'.

I had felt a strong spiritual energy on my first visit to this area, and each day it seemed to grow stronger. This accounted for my quick assumption in this regard. Many further occurrences simply reinforced my acceptance of this unexplainable, yet very real phenomenon. For those not sufficiently armed against 'Black Magic', these so-called coincidences could wreak havoc in their world. I learned to make a conscious decision to use my ultimate resource, God, to guard against these powers by creating a field of positive energy around myself. I fell into the habit of doing this whenever I felt negative vibrations around me.

"Ya ready to head out to the mine? If you could borrow Dick's truck, we could take in a couple loads tomorrow."

"I can hardly wait." I was finally going to get into the area I had been hearing so much about.

The next day we began the trip that was to become a regular part of my life for the next couple of years. The first step, of course, was to load the fuel drums, food for the camp and other mining gear into the two vehicles. WD's unit did not have a truck box, as it was a very old Toyota BJ45 model, fully roofed with seats in the back. Nevertheless, into the rear of it we rolled some fuel drums, and even threw in a couple of live chickens for good measure. No fridge out there, so fresh food was a luxury.

The first stop, about ten minutes out of town, was at a Guardia alcabala. All vehicles heading either west or east through this checkpoint met heavy scrutiny. These government forces strictly controlled the western territory, as a lot of it was Indian land, National park or environmentally protected. At each passing, miners were met with some especially gruelling inspections of their fuel permits and other paper work. These inspections were harshest on the way out, as the Guardia Nacional wanted the miners to declare all diamonds removed from the area. As the Guardia's connection with the Internal Revenue part of the government was dubious, to say the least, confiscation of the hard-earned, shiny stones presented a very real possibility. Declaring them at this point would be foolhardy, and a good way to loose the little profit made. Therefore, each trip past this point was cause for some trepidation.

"Well, made it through agin," WD said with a light chuckle. "They made me produce my pistol this time, along with the paper work for it. That's good, 'cuz now they know I have it. No doubt, any would be banditos will know it too. Gotta take care of yourself out here, and watch yur ass."

An hour of driving along a high-grade, gravel road had brought us out of the treeless, sabana type surroundings and into the lush jungle. The terrain now started getting hilly, and we stopped at a viewpoint overlooking the breathtaking, green canopy. An elusive Mynah bird sent his shrill cry across the valley, providing the soundtrack for this unforgettable picture. While I was enjoying this rare moment, WD was preoccupied with checking out his old beast, ensuring the motor was ready to handle the arduous leg of the journey ahead.

"From here on, we're on our own. Luke finished this trail about eight months ago. Before that, the only way into the concession was by coming in from the north during the dry season. Crossing the Kukenan River up there is an adventure you might get to see some day. The Pemon Indians who live here walked in or came by canoe, and many still do. Now, in the rainy season, this trail is hell, but it's the only way we can get in here at this time of the year. We'll head north from here, through a little Indian village called Betania, and then up over a mountain. We're gonna come to a real steep hill, so you stay back 'til I get over the top," WD warned me. "There's already been one truck go over the side."

The road was relatively good up to Betania where the new trail commenced. All knowledge gained in my years of off-roading was now put to the test. I watched as WD spun his way up the muddy ruts to the top of the infamous hill, and I just hoped that I was up to the task as well. The thirty-foot bank to my left was intimidating, so I hugged the ruts on the inner side of the trail. Unfortunately, I got a little too cozy with the hillside and spun out. Reluctant to start rocking the vehicle in this precarious position, WD came to my assistance by turning his vehicle around and winching me up to the top.

"You weren't kidding when you said this was hairy," I joked.

"You ain't seen nothin' yet," he said, with a slight smirk on his face.

Up we climbed into the most beautiful jungle landscape I had ever seen. The foliage at this higher elevation was far more impressive than that far below. Here there was an assortment of colour and a real variety of both plant and bird life. Crossing a small creek, we encountered a rabble of yellow butterflies so thick that I just had to stop and walk into their midst. They were attracted to some alkali on the road and were impervious to my intrusion. With hundreds of yellow fluttering creatures about me, I must have been some sight.

Our next challenge was a long mud hole into which numerous logs had been strategically placed. The goal was to hit this stretch fast, have the wheels mount the logs, and zip through to the other side. Great theory, but hard to accomplish. This time it was WD's turn to fall off the logs and into the mire. With no trees close enough for the winch to reach, it was time for the trusty old jack-all. Standing in mud up to our knees, we managed to jack his unit high enough to place some logs under the wheels. Once he was up and out, we placed the existing logs in a better position for me to target. This time I was successful; our adventure continued.

After many kilometres of successfully traversing mud-holes and creeks, we started downhill, and before long, we broke out of the jungle. The sky became visible once more. But now we were confronted with a new dilemma; an expanse of water about half a kilometre long.

"Follow me and you won't have any problem," exclaimed WD, viewing my apprehension.

"It seems to me I've heard that too often down here," I said, chuckling nervously.

In we went, with water splashing over the running boards, to the other side. While passing through this canal of water, I was shocked to see women on the side washing clothes. Even more astonishing was that they did not appear annoyed with the waves of dirty water we created in our wake. Instead, they greeted us with friendly waves and smiles. We drove up out of the 'laundromat' and onto the dirt plaza of Apoipo.

This small village of mud huts was still adjusting to the arrival of vehicles driving through the centre of their life. Not a common occurrence yet, it was reason for a large turn out of spectators. Children were especially attracted to our presence and started running alongside our trucks. While WD stopped to talk to one of the elders, I couldn't resist joining the kids in a game of soccer they had underway. This brought many laughs as they watched this strange, white man stumble and fall, chasing them and the ball around. A bond with the people of Apoipo began for me that day, and continued until I left the area a couple of years later.

"Well, now that we are through the easy part, I sure hope we can get through to the concession. This next section has a lot of log bridges that I hope are still there."

"You're kidding, aren't you?" I asked, not believing it could get worse than what we had just been over.

"You'll see," was all WD said.

We headed east out of the village, following a very muddy and water-covered trail. One minute we were under the canopy of the jungle, while the next found us in the wide-open sabana. But the trail remained consistent; it was demanding. Many spots required backing up several times before any forward progress could be made. Crossing the numerous log bridges tested my reflexes, as well as my nerves. These crossings consisted of three logs tied together for one set of wheels, and another trio for the other side. No room for error, as a plunge into a fast moving creek could be fatal. The final 'bridge' was to be my nemesis on future trips, as it spanned a canyon about ten metres deep and the approaches from both sides were usually slippery.

Now back out in the open savannah, a new terrain presented a different form of obstacle. Though grass covered, the ground was water logged at this time of year. Our plan involved speed. We had to cross this stretch as fast as possible, staying out of old tracks to reach the high ground on the other side. After crossing several sections successfully, my old Toyota finally succumbed to the beckoning mud. Now a real dilemma presented itself, as high ground was too far away for WD's winch to reach me. Here I was to learn an entirely new method of extraction. A small plant, resembling a miniature Joshua tree, and locally known as venado, was used to provide a base for the jack, and subsequently placed under the wheels and along the path ahead. This required a lot of work, but after a couple of hours, we finally got the vehicle to high ground. From that day forward, I dreaded trips across that area in the rainy season.

Now, about ten hours after we had left Sta. Elena, we finally arrived at the mining camp, a welcome site for both the miners and us. The miners were especially pleased to see us because their food supply was nearly gone.

"We're moving camp in the morning," WD told Maturin, the leader of the five man crew. "I've found another place that looks real promising. We'll have to load everything on the trucks, drive down to the water and load it on a raft. We'll float it across to the other side."

My companion didn't waste anytime mincing words, even in Spanish. No one questioned his decision, even though the crew had a fifty per cent stake in the outcome. After all, he was providing the food on credit in these lean times, and it had been some time since they had had a good 'clean-up'. Diamonds had been elusive as of late.

We hung our hammocks in the tin shack just as darkness overtook us. The cook prepared a meal of boiled meat and rice as we sat about the campfire sharing the latest news from the outside. After a hard day of exercise, it didn't take me long to fall into a deep sleep in this very serene setting.

Even before breakfast, the men started dismantling the camp and loading everything onto the truck. Securing the corrugated tin panels, water pipes, hoses and other mining paraphernalia onto the vehicles took some ingenuity. It all had to be tied in well with ropes, as the rough trail to the river was not about to give us a reprieve. As soon as breakfast was devoured, off we went.

When we arrived at the water's edge, I'm sure my eyes must have looked like the were bulging out of their sockets. This was no river; it was a huge lake! The river had overflowed its banks and now covered the whole plain in front of us. Where the actual stream lay, I had no idea; after all, this was my first time into this valley.

The men quickly assembled a raft using empty fuel drums and wooden planks. The tough job of loading the heavy, mining equipment onto the raft began. With the added weight, it became very difficult to get the raft out from shore into water deep enough for it to float. With an immense amount of manpower, tugging and pulling, we soon had the raft on its way over to the far shore with its first load of cargo. Repeated trips throughout the day perfected our system, and by days end, camp, fuel drums, mining jig (approximately three-hundred kilos), two pumps (another three-hundred kilos each), pipes, hose, and the rest of the gear found itself on the opposite shore. The miners manhandled the pumps and jig by mounting and exchanging two wheels between the heavy items. Not one load tipped into the water; this alone was a fait accompli.

At about five o'clock in the afternoon, the heavens opened up. This, I was informed, was quite normal at this time of year. The amount of rain that fell in the next hour or so would have been more than a month's normal rainfall at home. It came down so hard it literally hurt the face and body as we hastily reassembled the camp. Finally sheltered from this torrential downpour, we stood inside listening to the rain battering the tin roof. Fortunately, we had a propane stove, so supper could be prepared inside our protective hut.

The next morning, WD showed the crew where he wanted them to start mining. Hopes of a good clean-up of diamonds was high on everyone's agenda. To safeguard his part, WD placed a lock on the metal covering of the jig; this was where trust ended. The extraction of precious gems would have to wait until his return.

While wading through water on the way back to our vehicle, I struggled to comprehend all I had just experienced. My muscles were also struggling, aching all over from the unaccustomed physical stresses they had just been subjected to. Our return to town was just as eventful as it had been coming out. Soon, these trips would simply become the normal order of things.

This trip had allowed me to learn a bit about the man that eventually would become my very close friend and partner in many ventures. Watching how he dealt with situations and people impressed me immensely. In my hunt for a viable person to team up with, I was looking for someone with both sincerity and integrity. It appeared my search was over.

Now that the future was starting to become a little clearer, it was time to deal with another matter. Up until now, I had little time to think about my newfound love sitting up in Maturin. Now, the lonely heart started making its inattention known. It was time to get serious, take root, establish myself and start a new home.

Chapter 21

"**G**O FOR IT. You'd be a fool not to take this opportunity," I told Liz over the phone. She had just completed a college course in Multi Media Broadcasting and was now in a quandary. A talent scout from the big city had come by and offered her an audition for a position with their TV station.

"I don't want to live in Caracas," replied Liz in Spanish. "I don't know anybody there, and wouldn't have a place to live. Besides, I want to come to Sta. Elena with you. Maybe I can work for the radio station there."

My subsequent arguments lost vigour as Liz's adamant persuasion of her feelings coupled with my own. Yes, sharing life with this vibrant young 'chica' in the Gran Sabana was not a hard concept to digest. The fact that she was willing to go to such lengths to be with this cash strapped gringo quelled any doubts of her motives.

With that phone call securing our relationship, I rented a tourist cabin and headed north to pick up Liz. Two days and eight hundred miles later, we were both nestled into our new home in Sta. Elena. Nicely tucked into the corner of a tourist compound, this one room bungalow was totally fenced in and secure. With the purchase of a fridge, stove and bed, we were set.

Our neighbour within this enclosure had a truly mean dog named Samson, who added a strong deterrent to potential intruders. This Brazilian Mastiff, a brown mass of muscle, controlled all entries into our area. He took particular exception to my ragged mining hat, so

I always had to remember to remove it before entering the yard. It took about two months before Samson allowed me to pet him, even though he would often curl up at my feet on the patio. This strange dog also held some secrets in the family closet.

One evening, upon returning to our little abode, Liz informed me that the lights had been going on and off without reason. I checked the switches and power sources and could see nothing out of the ordinary. Then, suddenly, one light went out. After a few minutes, it came back on and another one went off. This continued for about a half an hour, first one light, and then another. Just when we thought we would go crazy, the lights all came on and this erratic behaviour stopped.

A couple of evenings later, as we sat eating supper, an ashtray crashed to the floor. We both felt a very strong presence of someone else in the room; it was as if someone or something was seriously trying to get our attention. The sudden blast of the stereo turning on brought us both right out of our seats. This was getting serious. Once more, the lights started their on and off routine. I looked at Liz and was shocked to see a two-inch aura of white from the top of her head to her shoulders. Now fully aware of the power within the room, my feelings were not of fear, but rather a strong sense of curiosity. Soon the paranormal scene evaporated; the aura disappeared and strong vibrations in the room mellowed out.

I was lucky that Liz knew, as I did, how spirits sometimes become entrapped, and we were sure that this was the situation we presently faced. Filled with compassion for this lost soul, we decided to seek help. And, of course, it would be nice to get our privacy back!

When I mentioned this to WD, he suggested I look up an English-speaking friend of his, named Lefty, whom he believed would be able to shed some light on these mystifying occurrences. Eagerly, I called the number he gave me.

"Lefty, I have a question for you. Do you know anything about the cabin we're living in? It's in that tourist spot down by the river."

"I know the place. What do you mean?" he asked.

"Well, I think we might have a spirit or ghost hanging around.

There are some pretty weird things going on."

"Well, it's interesting you should say that. There's definitely some history on that place. The owners had their daughter staying in the cabin you're in now, with her six-year-old son. The father of Samson, the dog next door, was their pet. Tragically, one day the dog attacked and killed the young boy. No one knows why or what happened."

"Wow, that explains a lot! Now we have to do something. Where can I find out the boys name and other facts?"

"My wife up in Pto. Odaz was involved in trying to help the family. Maybe you should go up there and talk to her."

Before coming to South America, I had read a series of books written by Mary Summer Rain. She wrote of some things that had also occurred in my life, ones that had no scientific explanation. The character of 'No Eyes' in her first book, Spirit Song, had helped me to become more open about my own out of body journey, my ability to sense ghosts and other unexplainable events. I felt confident that my knowledge and first hand experience in these matters would be beneficial in this matter; especially as I recalled how Mary Summer Rain had dealt with such circumstances in one of her books, Phantoms Afoot. I suspected that the young lad's spirit had not evolved the way it should have. However, I needed more information.

"I can arrange to borrow a vehicle to go north. Do you want to come for a ride, Lefty?"

"Sure. I'm not doing much these days anyway. Would be nice to get home for a visit."

So, a few days later, Liz, Lefty and I started the nine hour trip north to Pto Odaz. On the way, Lefty introduced me to another spiritual path; it was in the form of a book called Autobiography of a Yogi. This introduction to Paramahansa Yogananda was the beginning of a spiritual path I later pursued wholeheartedly. However, I still had a few reality checks to face before I could open my soul to that wise guru's insight.

"So, please tell me the story about the young boy in the cabin," I said to Lefty's wife, as I pulled a chair up to her kitchen table. Lefty had explained our purpose by phone before we arrived.

"His name was Carlos. The dog attacked him when the mother went outside for a moment. When she heard the screaming, she ran inside and tried to pull the dog off Carlos, but it was too late. They rushed him to the hospital, but he was dead on arrival."

Though she spoke in Spanish, I could feel the strong emotion in her voice as she retold this story.

"The family was in terrible grief, both the Grandparents and the mother. The boy's father wasn't around. After the incident, the family constantly felt the presence of the young lad around their home, like his spirit or something. That's when they contacted me."

"Why did they do that?"

"People in the community knew that I had dealt with wayward spirits in the past, and felt I might be able to help them. So, I talked to the family, and let them know that by their heavy grieving and crying, they were actually holding Carlos back from carrying on to his rightful place in heaven."

Lefty's wife paused and stared out the window in silence. We all remained quiet and let her gather herself. It had obviously been a very traumatic time for her.

"I suggested we gather in what is now your cabin," she continued, "and with the whole family in deep meditation, we sent out a message to young Carlos that it was ok for him to carry on. I thought we had been successful, but it appears not."

"Well, I appreciate what you've been through. What do you think we should do?"

For the next while, we discussed various means of helping Carlos escape the confines of our less than perfect world. Thanking Lefty's wife profusely, we told her we would keep her informed of how we made out, and may call if we had any further questions. She wished us well, and we returned home the next day.

Back in our little abode, Liz and I prepared to assist our small spiritual friend make his final departure. Although I definitely lacked the experience of my mentor, Mary Summer Rain, I still felt very confident in what we were about to undertake.

Candles lit and incense burning, we settled into a quiet repose. Slowly, we both allowed our restlessness to dissipate, and entered into another realm of consciousness. Through partially closed eyes, I could once again see the aura around Liz's being. It was not long thereafter that I could sense another presence in our midst. I gently started cultivating and then projecting feelings of peace and love outwardly, with a mental message directed to Carlos.

"It's okay Carlos, you can go now. You have no reason to stay here anymore. Go." I repeated this over and over in Spanish. "It's okay Carlos, you can go now. You have no reason to stay here anymore. Go."

After an unknown length of time, his presence slowly drifted away. Gradually I returned to the reality of our time and space, feeling a sense of calm I had not felt in years. When Liz joined me once more in this realm, we shared what had just transpired; I found that she had gone through the same process as I had, and now had the same rewarding feelings of peace. There was no doubt – Carlos had left the building.

With that diversion out of the way, life took on new dimensions. Liz got a job as a teacher's aid, and I resumed my freelance work. More trips to the mine with WD had me gaining some real insight into this whole diamond mining process. One of the first things I had to learn was what a diamond in the rough really looked like. The hardest part for me was keeping my hands out of the jig when the men were doing a clean-up. My ignorance readily showed whenever I gasped at the sight of shiny, quartz crystals. The crew was quick to notice this. They tried to take advantage of my ignorance by slipping real diamonds into their mouths or between their fingers while I was distracted by the false glimmer. My job was to watch them, and not look for the diamonds. After a few successful clean-ups, I came to recognize a diamond by its 'life'. There is no other way to describe them, and it is truly a thrill to see the glitter coming forth from amidst the rocks, sand and quartz.

The process of extracting these diamonds was another learning curve. Two diesel water pumps were used, the first one providing water for hydraulic mining. This entailed using a high-pressure water hose to blast the terrain and wash the material into a waiting suction hose. The second pump moved this material up to a water-propelled apparatus called a jig. The force of water activated a diaphragm that levitated the material, as well as setting in motion the oscillating action required to move the diamonds to the bottom of the gravel. With the diamonds and gold settling to the bottom, the lighter material fell out into a chute, flowing down a small sluice-box. A locked metal plate on top kept 'light fingers' out, although there was no way to secure the sluice. The clean-up of this material was usually done every three or four days, depending on when the 'boss' arrived with the key.

As there was neither rhyme nor reason to where these diamonds might lie, it was always a point of contention where to mine next. No kimberlite pipes or any trace of one had ever been found in this area. This fact caused a slight ethical problem for me. As a freelancer, I wrote stock market reports for several miners. One of these was a Canadian working on the Codza concession.

"You have me typing in your report here Martin, that you have just found a kimberlite pipe. You know, and I know, that there aren't any out there. What's with this?"

"We have to keep the stockholders happy; that's what they want to see," Martin replied. "They're our bread and butter until we hit the big one."

"So, how do you sleep at night knowing that you may have just conned some little old lady out of her life's savings?" I asked, visibly showing my displeasure with such deception.

"Well, she should be savvy enough if she is playing the stock market. That isn't my responsibility," was his curt response.

I was learning that there were three main camps diametrically opposed to one another, and I was walking the fine line between them all. There were the Americans, Canadians and the Venezuelan/Guayanese/Brazilian group. In addition, there were those that worked and acted totally apart from everyone else. I found myself working for all these parties, gaining their trust, yet maintaining my independence.

"Ron, I need to slip up to Canada for a few weeks. Can I get you to take care of things for me while I am gone?" asked my friend Dick.

"No problem, just tell me what you want and I'll take care of it."

On that note, Dick and family left for Canada, and I assumed watch over his holdings. Not long after he was gone, I noticed that his number one man had been robbing him blind, and was quite blatant in doing so. To ward off a serious confrontation, I suggested he take a break, and go to his home in Maracaibo for a vacation.

When Dick returned, I pointed out what Marco had been up to, suggesting that it would be wise to get rid of him. Dick readily agreed but the method was going to be tricky. Marco was from the oil country in the east, and would be quite versed in his rights under the labour act. With this in mind, Dick brought his lawyer along when it came time to deal with Marco.

Sure enough, when confronted, Marco wanted a severance package.

"How can you ask for anything? You owe me!" yelled Dick.

"You have no right to fire me like this without any notice," Marco retorted in Spanish. "I want ten thousand B's severance."

"No damn way," stormed Dick.

"Let's go outside for a minute," the lawyer suggested, motioning to both Dick and me.

Once outside, the lawyer continued, "This is more complicated than you think. In this country, it is more serious to accuse someone of theft than thievery itself. You would be far ahead to pay up now. Believe me, he can cause you a lot of grief."

We returned inside and an agreement was drawn up, which required Marco to leave the area upon receipt of his money. Only in Venezuela could one be rewarded for stealing.

It appeared that I had not yet escaped from the northern, labour idiocy. My hope was that this would conclude, once and for all, that chapter of my life. Thankfully, it did. Everyone learnt a good lesson, and special precautions were implemented to thwart any future incursion of labour militants. However, there was another Venezuelan blight known as embargoes. These would plague the whole industry, eventually causing the demise of many. These occurred when a person would put a lean on another's equipment. Often the basis for these caveats was one hundred per cent false, procured by a pay off to an obliging judge. Corruption at its finest.

One ex-pat who had managed to survive these complications was a local diamond buyer, and fellow miner, named Floyd. An ex-military pilot from the Second World War, he moved from Texas to Central America in the late forties. A book could be written of his many exploits piloting various aircraft throughout Latin America. He settled in Guyana where he did quite well for a while. Political unrest caused his sudden departure from there, and even worse, the loss of his plane. Now settled here in Venezuela, he had become a bit of a local legend. He was approaching his eightieth birthday, although one would never know it.

"I'm going out to the mine tomorrow Ron. Care to team up?" Floyd asked.

"Sure. I was planning on heading out tomorrow too. The road's real bad right now, so travelling together would be a great idea."

We got an early morning start, and as expected, the road was a challenge. Floyd took the lead, and we winched and jacked our way through the numerous waterholes. I was amazed at the stamina of this elderly man, as he sloshed through the mud pulling my winch cable to his truck.

Our arrival in Apoipo seemed to be cause for excitement, as the whole town turned out to block our path. My first reaction was that we had somehow upset the natives over something. I sat nervously in the truck, while they had words with Floyd up front.

Floyd slowly got out of his truck and sauntered back to mine.

"Ron, seems that an old gal died last night, and the folks want us to take the coffin and a bunch of 'em up to the graveyard. I'll take the coffin in the back of my truck, if you can load a bunch of the elders into yours."

"Sounds good to me," I said, and began loading people in through the back door of the old Toyota. Soon we were on our way, with people hanging all over both Floyd's truck and mine. We now found ourselves chauffeurs in a funeral parade. How quickly the logistics of a trip could change.

A few days later, I was once more sipping coffee at the panadaria in town, when Dick sat down and asked,

"Ron, how would you like to go into Polaco?"

"Well, you know gringos aren't too welcome there. That's an association of local miners," I replied.

"Yea, I know. My Brazilian friend Francisco has an operation in Polaco, and I'm lending him some equipment. Maybe we can get our foot in there somehow. A lot of diamonds have come out of there."

"What the heck, you know me, always ready for a new adventure."

With that said, plans were made for me to venture into a very remote area that few white people had ever set foot. This would turn out to be a trip that I certainly would not volunteer for a second time.

Chapter 22

THE LURE OF gold and diamonds has a way of infiltrating the very soul of men. I found myself slowly succumbing to this fever. Tales of a fourteen carat diamond found in the Polaco region found me joining the latest 'bulla' (diamond rush). We loaded and tied down Francisco's equipment on Dick's Toyota, securing the long irrigation pipes, fuel drums, and a lot of food for the men. This load was about to be subjected to an unforgiving ride into the jungle that would test even a sailor's knot. The journey into Polaco began by passing through the infamous alcabala, heading west from Sta. Elena. After a couple of hours, we turned off the main road and aimed south towards the Brazilian border. After an extra cinching of ropes around the fuel drums and pipes, we ventured forth on a well-worn trail.

"How far in from here is it Francisco?"

"Depends," he replied smiling. "It all depends. If the trail is good and the truck doesn't break down, maybe two hours. There have been trips that have taken me two days to get in, so, who knows?"

From the very outset, the trail opposed us, with only skilled mud bogging getting us through the first stretch. This brought us to the base of a steep, rocky hill. As I analyzed the degree of challenge ahead, one thing became certain; I didn't need to worry about slipping off the edge. Two deep grooves formed a guide to the top, so my main concern would be to keep the undercarriage of the truck intact. We rocked our way forth up this mini-canyon, scraping and grinding along the rocky surface. When one side of the truck was lower than the opposite, the racks on the truck box scraped along the unforgiving canyon of stone. First on one side, then the other. With four wheels grasping for whatever grip they could find, and the undercarriage grinding along the hump in the middle of the trail, we inched our way upward. There was no option but to remain in the ruts, proceed forward and pray we didn't break anything. I was grateful that no one chose that time to come down the hill, as there was no room to pass. Seems there were not a lot of fools like us travelling this trail. For more than an hour this abuse of man and machine continued, until we finally crested a hill, devoid of trees. Far below, the settlement of Polaco lay spread out before us.

"Is this the only way down?" I asked Francisco. "The brakes on this truck aren't very reliable."

"I'm afraid so," he replied. "Just stay to the inside, and keep it in low gear. If it slides or the brakes fail, run the truck up against the bank. We sure don't want to fall off the other side."

And with that, we started our descent. It is without shame that I confess I was scared out of my mind! Muddy, narrow and steep, with sharp curves and a sheer bank off the right side, there was no room for error, or other vehicles. With careful navigation, we successfully reached the settlement, my heart thumping fiercely every bit of the way.

We then entered a tin shack community that was like a step back in time. As there were few vehicles in the settlement, there was only a system of pathways connecting the various services, which included a crude laundry, open-air restaurants and tin-roofed stores. It was like a scene out of the Klondike gold rush.

We spent the night in Francisco's hut, and started down the footpath to the mining area first thing in the morning. The trail followed the river, and being too narrow for vehicles, the miners packed all their gear in by hand.

"Do you believe in ghosts?" Francisco inquired.

"Yes, why do you ask?"

"Well, there's one who appears around here after dark. She's a blonde, white woman who guards this passage religiously. You won't find a miner around here who'll come past this spot after the sun goes down."

"Does she appear evil or seem to threaten anyone?" I asked.

"No, and nobody knows where she came from, or why she's hanging around here." Francisco's serious demeanour confirmed his strong belief in this ghostly spirit.

"I'd like to see her. Do you want to come back here with me tonight?"

"Not a chance, Ron, and I don't think you'll find anyone else that will either."

Later on, I tried to convince several miners to join me on a ghostly adventure, but Francisco had been right; there were no takers.

The next morning we made our way to the mining area and my eyes were greeted by total chaos. There seemed to be no set divisions, with miners hosing down the banks wherever they felt there might be diamonds lurking. Rivulets of water flowed everywhere, winding their way back to the murky river. No settling ponds or other environmental controls here! I felt excitement growing as we approached the area where that 'granddaddy of all diamonds' had been unearthed.

With a slow look around, I observed that the only unmolested piece of land in the area was a huge mound of tree covered terrain about fifty metres high. This amount of overburden, lying on top of the diamond-bearing material, was formidable, and obviously why it was still untouched. My heart began to sink as reality set in. Even if we could find a way to work in here with this association of Venezuelan miners, where would we work?

We made our way to where Francisco's crew was working. They had been having one problem after another, making little, if any, progress. Then, while we stood there watching them blast a bank of dirt with the high-pressure water, one of his men started screaming and jumping around. Another miner grabbed the hose from him while the agitated miner scrambled out of the water onto shore. Like a man possessed, he tore his pants off and out crawled the largest black scorpion I had ever seen. When we examined his leg, we discovered that the scorpion had stung him three times. Once we had the man calmed down, the poison slowly made its way through his system without any major effect. He was back on the end of a high-pressure hose in less than an hour.

The next day we departed, taking with us parts needing repair and production shut down once more. Even under normal conditions, mining is no easy task; the obstacles presented here were just too plentiful to warrant a return.

After the Polaco fiasco, WD challenged me with another daunting proposal.

"Ron, how would you like to go on another adventure?"

"Lay it on me. What have you got in mind?"

"I have a small dredge down on the Cuyuni River by Kilometre 88. The men running it haven't sent me any money, yet I know they're finding gold. I want you to spend some time with them and find out what's goin' on," WD said, his irritation showing in his voice.

I left for what was to be an eight-day excursion deep into the low elevation jungle of central Venezuela. This type of tropical forest was far different from that found in the higher altitude of the Gran Sabana. This hot and humid region had all sorts of unpleasantries waiting: malaria bearing mosquitoes, poisonous snakes and a river full of hungry piranhas to name but a few.

The crew met me in KM 88, and we headed up the river on the small dredge. This flat bottom craft was equipped with a diesel motor, huge suction pump, sluice, compressor for the divers and all the necessities of life away from civilization. We headed deep into the forest, with the intent of going far beyond the other miners. I would not hear or speak English for the next week or so.

A full day of travelling down stream brought us close to where we planned to work. During the course of our journey, I gradually became aware that I was an unwelcome guest, and attempts at frightening me had begun.

"Last night, one of the miners got stabbed up here," the crew captain told me.

"What was that about."

"Over an ounce of gold. We all share production out here, and the crew was trying to cheat the guy. When he argued, they killed him." The look in the captain's eyes reinforced my belief that he was trying to intimidate me. He had not yet learned that I was normally the intimidator, not the other way around.

It had been obvious from the start that these men did not want me with them. They had a slick little operation going, using WD's equipment to make a huge profit with little overhead. One thing they did not want was for me to report just how lucrative it really was. We were now truly in a no-man zone, where the law of the jungle was the prevailing force. The dynamics of the situation compelled me to assume my 'loco gringo' routine. With some creative language and bizarre actions, I soon smashed any preconceptions they may have had of me. Once I had successfully established myself as being a bit crazy, I was able to close the second eye when I slept. The only companion I had out here was a gift from a friend, the 9 mm handgun stashed in my backpack.

In the morning, we broke away from the main river, and proceeded up a small tributary that the dredge could barely negotiate. Now we really were alone, no other boats or miners had any inclination to explore this far into the depths of the jungle. When the time arrived to tie up and start working, my advice as to where we should work was ignored. Their scheme was obvious: deliberately set up in spots they knew we would not recover any gold, thus they wouldn't have to share any of their prosperity. By sucking up useless gravel, they would prove to me how hard it was to find gold here. They grossly underestimated my knowledge and experience. I knew what type of places this allusive, heavy metal would settle into, and they were about to find that out.

Our diet for the whole week was to be piranha and rice. On the third day, an Indian came by in a canoe and I spotted that he had some oranges; fruit never tasted so good. He also had some cigarettes. I had left the smokes behind, hoping to quit, knowing there would be no stores out here. So much for that idea. Some quick negotiation had me back puffing, which certainly did help to take the edge off my raw nerves. Yes, what a welcome relief that was.

Gold mining generates a unique form of insanity in some people, and these underwater-miners had to possess their share of it to carry out their task. The divers would submerse themselves into the dark, murky water for up to ten hours at a time. With only a wet suit and no light to guide them, they held on to the end of the suction hose, while it ate away at the river bottom. In doing so, they often created sheer walls of gravel that often caved in, trapping them in a watery grave. The deadly electric eel was another formidable peril. Stories abounded of how divers had been jolted into the next world by these dangerous little creatures.

"I want to take a crack at it," I told the crew captain one day.

"Are you sure?" he asked, as he went on to chronicle the dangers emphatically. None of them had ever seen a gringo dive here, and this just added to their uncertainty about me. This, of course, suited me just fine.

"Yes, suit me up." I donned the wet suit, put on my mask and inserted the regulator mouthpiece. An air hose connected my regulator to the compressor on deck. With a safety rope attached, I followed the suction hose down to the bottom, and when they started up the pump, I began guiding the nozzle along the river bottom. I soon found myself blindly feeling my way around, as the water became too murky to see anything. Twenty minutes of that unsettling work was all I could endure. Now I was certain; these miners had to be crazed to remain down there for such long periods.

I was constantly monitoring the crew's attitude, always being careful not to cross them too severely. My insistence on dredging where I wanted was a real point of contention. After several unsuccessful clean ups, they relented and positioned the dredge where I suggested. We moved to a bend in the river, and as I expected, we finally recovered eight ounces of gold. Alas, this was the only production WD was ever to see from this crew.

On our way back to civilization, we stopped at a native community on the edge of the river. These very hospitable people fed us a decent meal of chicken, yucca, and vegetables, topped off with fresh fruit. What a delightful change from the diet of bony fish and plain rice we had been living on for the past week.

As we were getting ready to leave the village, I joined the chief under the shade of a huge tree, where we became engaged in a delightful conversation. That is, until his eyes started looking over my shoulder and he unsheathed his machete. I froze. The chief's eyes seemed to relay my degree of danger. He slowly brought his blade up by my right shoulder, which just happens to be adjacent to my neck. I immediately thought, "Oh my God, what did I say to piss him off!"

He gave a quick, yet gentle flick with the dull side of the blade on my shoulder, and then he pointed to the ground. I hesitantly allowed my head to move and shifted my gaze down. There, quickly scurrying away, was what was commonly known as a twenty-four-hour ant. These huge, reddish-black insects inflict a severely painful sting, whose venom causes effects similar to that of malaria. Fortunately, when afflicted, the victim only suffers for about a day, thus the reason for the ant's label. I thanked my protector profusely, although I'm sure he had a slight chuckle at the fear he must have seen in my eyes.

On my return, WD shut down that operation and sold the dredge. It was just too hard to keep control of an operation that far away. After seeing all these failures, my faith in the mining business was starting to wane. WD picked up on that and said,

"Ron, we had a pretty good clean up when you were gone. I'm going over to Floyds to sell some diamonds. C'mon."

When we walked into Floyd's house, there was another miner selling his sparkling goods. He had his success spread out on a black velvet cloth and was busy taking pictures of them. With about ten thousand dollars worth of diamonds staring back at me, the dream didn't seem quite so impossible anymore. WD sold his diamonds, and as we were saying our good-byes, I noticed a painting on the wall. The scene was one of a leprechaun like being sitting on the edge of a tepui.

"What's that?" I asked Floyd.

"That was painted by Walter, an old guy who wanders about the sabana. When I asked him that same question, he told me that if I kept my mind and eyes open a little more, I might be surprised by what I saw out there. He was deadly serious when he said that."

"Well, I guess I'll have to try that too," I said with a chuckle. My sceptical mind wasn't quite ready for 'fairy tales' yet, but it was being opened more and more each day.

With Christmas coming soon, Liz and I decided to head north to visit her family for the holidays. I was about to finally meet them. They lived in Tucupita, on the delta of the Orinoco. With a long drive ahead of us, we borrowed Tom's truck and headed north.

On the way, we stopped in the small town of Baranca to visit Liz's grandparents. Here, two elderly people, one of them blind, invited us in to their very modest home with open hearts. This couple was so happy and content, and with so little. This was a very humbling experience for me, as these seniors were at peace with their lot in life and felt no desire to chase gold or diamonds to improve on it. I left yearning to have more of what these sincere and delightful people had – pure contentment. I asked Liz,

"How do they eat? There is no stove, cupboards or anything there. A bed, chairs, and that is all. I saw a forty-five gallon drum in the corner. What was that for?"

"The neighbours bring them food everyday. Sometimes, if it gets a bit cold, they burn wood in the drum to keep warm; they even cook food over it. I would really like them to move up close to Mom, but they don't want to. They like it right where they're at." That was obvious, I thought to myself, although Liz didn't seem to share my evaluation of the scene.

In Tucupita, we booked into the only western style motel I was to see in the whole country. A new building with a large pool and about seventy rooms, it was a real oddity in this area. It would have been out of character anywhere in the country, but especially here.

My apprehension was intense when we arrived at the home of Liz's parents. I was twenty-three years older than their daughter, was a foreigner, and not overly affluent. These fears were quickly dispelled when I learned that Tito, Liz's dad, was twenty years older than Egda, his wife, making our age disparity a non-issue. Moreover, I spoke Spanish and was providing their youngest with a home. Thus, the reception they gave me was one of a family member.

Once a middle class family, these people had lived in near poverty since the fall of the Perez government. Liz's mother had worked for the administration, but since retirement, had been waiting for years of back pay owed to her. Although part of the office staff, she had been requested by President Perez to cook for him each time he came to town; her cooking was renowned throughout the community.

Children filled the confines of the small home, as Liz's older sisters had a habit of having children, then leaving them with 'Abuela' to raise. I soon became attached to all of them, but in particular to a young boy about eight-years old, ironically named Ronaldo. His mother had gone through a divorce, so he now lived with his grandmother and his cousins. Another charmer was Magdellan, a mentally impaired young girl about thirteen-years old. It soon became apparent that Magdellan was relegated to many of the household tasks. At times there were as many as seven children filling the house with their constant laughter.

Tito's passion was his roosters. He allowed them in the house, and their constant crowing at all hours was something I had trouble getting used to. I joked about dining on 'rooster a la king', but Tito insisted that he knew what time it was by their crowing. They were his very own and personable 'cluck-cluck clock'.

"I'd like to take the kids to the pool," I told Liz.

"Okay, but it is going to be hard to control them all," she replied with a laugh. When we had the kids all ready to go, one was missing.

"Where's Magdellan?" I asked.

"Oh, you can't take her out in a public place. You know, with her being like she is and all," one of the sisters blurted.

"I'm sorry then," I said, "Because if she can't come, I'm not going."

This shocked everyone, because local custom was to keep handicapped people hidden from the stares of the outside world. Liz's sisters strongly contested my intentions, but I stood my ground. Magdellan came with us and had the time of her life. The kids behaved super and it was not only a highlight of Christmas for them, but for me as well.

After we had completed our wonderful holiday with this gracious family, we returned to our little abode in Sta Elena. Soon after our arrival home, I received a phone call from my son that was to add a new and exciting chapter to our lives.

Chapter 23

"Dad, I want to come down there to live with you." My son's request came totally out of the blue, catching me off guard. It was also a dream come true. The timing was not the best, but we had to make this work somehow. I was strapped for cash, and my living accommodations were meagre to say the least. Once again, my parents came to the rescue, and provided the funds for Shaine's plane trip down. Now, all I had to do was somehow fit him into our world. Nothing could have made me happier than this pleasant disruption of our lives. Even Liz was excited, although, she wasn't quite sure where I expected Shaine to sleep.

The seventeen-year old found himself once again travelling solo on a plane south from Calgary, through Dallas and Miami and on to Caracas. He was about to begin the biggest adventure of his lifetime. Had he known that in the next few months he would be incarcerated, have an attempt made on his life, and encounter numerous grave situations in the jungle, he might very well have re-boarded the plane. What he was about to gain though, was an experience very few his age could equal, and an exceptional transition into manhood.

"Welcome to Venezuela. Hope you're ready for this." I said laughing.

"Oh yeah, I could hardly wait to get here."

We flew down to the Gran Sabana, Shaine once more subjected to the 'delight' of flying on a DC-3. Flying on this old bird always seemed to make him a little green around the gills.

Cordialities out of the way, we slung a hammock up inside our little room. Liz, of course, wasn't all to sure what to make of everything. Since she didn't speak English, Liz felt left out of the conversation most of the time; it didn't take long to see that this living arrangement wasn't going to work.

"I'm going see if Dick will let you work for him for board and room until we get more established. Will that be okay with you?" I asked Shaine.

"Whatever," was his all too typical teen-age reply.

Sheila had returned to Canada with Loretta, and Michael had chosen to stay behind to help Dick. This was good for Shaine, for he not only had a place to work and live, but now he also had a friend about his age who spoke English.

In the months preceding Shaine's arrival, Liz and I had slowly blended into the community. I had come to know most of the major players in the mining game, had forged some new alliances, and had come to know who to beware of. Dick and I had a bond of friendship that extended back to our hometown of Peace River. Although he dabbled in the mining field, his main focus was on his restaurant and bar. I had my sights on diamonds.

I now appreciated my decision to wait and see who to join forces with. Slowly, I had come to know W.D. Allen. There wasn't a person in town who didn't know him, and he was always well spoken of. The first time I drove his old Toyota into town, it created a lot of murmuring in the street, as no one drove the finicky beast other than WD. This alone affirmed that Allen must have been gaining faith in me too.

W.D. Allen had moved to Venezuela about ten years before I arrived. Raised in Oklahoma, he had a mining degree that he had attained in Colorado. However, more important than his credentials, was his vision. Always game to try something new, he had taken on a variety of endeavours before my arrival. From a large dredging operation to a horseback tour company, his ventures had been interesting, if not exactly profitable. A very trusting soul, the last decade had withered his confidence in people somewhat, especially after numerous occurrences such as the one I had just experienced on the Rio Cuyuni.

I spent many enjoyable hours sitting and chatting with him on the deck of his comfortable home, his lovely wife Maria keeping us well supplied with iced lemonade. It was on one of those occasions that WD updated me on a new development.

"Ron, I've got some people coming down here from Tennessee who want to take a crack at diamond mining. They'll be bringing some heavy equipment and a bunch of personal effects." Leaning back in the easy chair on WD's veranda, I slowly absorbed the significance of what was transpiring.

"Going to be quite an undertaking bringing equipment in. I did that for two years and I know all too well the hassles involved with importation," I replied.

"Yeah, I know. But we should be able to make some good production once we get it here. They are bringing a small cat, a track-hoe and a front-end loader. We'll be able to move lotsa material with all that iron."

"Well, as you know, I've been working here and there for everyone, but I really would like to throw in with you completely if that's possible. I like how you operate, and you've been the one guy here that has given me a fair shake on everything I've done," I said.

Once I made the decision to team up with WD, he lent me enough equipment to start a crew of my own. With Shaine working for Dick, and Liz busy teaching, I set off for the Codza concession.

There I discovered a beautiful and secluded spot that would become my 'paradise.' I consulted with the local Pemon Indians, and they had no objection to me squatting on their land. For a half a case of rum, they would even build my hut. This would be the first, and only, mortgage-free home I would ever own.

Construction was slow to begin, and I could not figure out why they were procrastinating. The full ration of rum wasn't to be paid until the hut was complete, yet they kept saying, 'mas tarde' (later). I persisted nagging them, until they succumbed to my wishes.

However, they got the last laugh on this stubborn developer.

The men set about cutting the leaves of the Moriche palm, which became the only source of shelter for my new home. Since cutting this tree was not permitted, the Pemon use a machete attached to a long pole to cut the branches. We hauled several truckloads of Moriche palm branches to my site, and my new home began to take shape.

The spot I had chosen was ideal. The 'churuata' was constructed far from the main trail, in the open grassland. A pathway led ten metres into the jungle to a crystal-clear creek. The water flowed through a series of 'punch bowls', creating perfectly smooth, natural and tranquil bathtubs. Instead of incense, candles or potpourri, I was soothed by the flutter of large, blue butterflies, the whistle of Macaws and the sweet perfume of clean air. The setting was truly idyllic. And, if I chose to have a shower instead, just a little up-stream was a waterfall with a rock bench to sit on. Life just didn't get any better than this!

With my thatched roof complete, I slung my hammock and set-tled in to enjoy my new home. In the middle of the night, I awak-ened to a strange sound resonating from my new roof – a 'chewing' sound. With a flashlight I probed the darkness, hoping to find the source of this incessant munching, but to no avail.

"I think I've got bugs in my roof," I told one of the natives.

He laughed and said,

"We told you to wait. When you pick the leaves during a full moon, the little 'bollweevil' are fully active. If you had waited until there was no moon, there would be no bugs. Now you will have to soak your roof with salt-water."

I wasted no time in mixing up some salt and water, spraying the roof and ridding myself of the little pests before they literally ate me out of house and home.

With my bush-camp now established, I proceeded to employ a crew of local natives for my diamond mining operation. I felt that this would improve our relations with them, as our encroachment on their land was rapidly becoming contentious. The government-granted concession to work here was legal, but consideration of the needs and desires of the native population had to be taken into account. I hoped to smooth the waters somewhat, a decision that was to have serious ramifications later on.

While searching for a place to commence mining, my crew suggested a spot they knew well. It was an area used only by the Indians for recovering diamonds, and they had been working there for years. I hesitated about entering this area, as the concession holder deemed it off limits. After some persuasion, the crew convinced me to move the operation there anyway.

When I arrived with the first load of equipment on the truck, there were two native women standing where we intended to start our operation.

"What are you doing?" they asked as I pulled up.

"We're going to set up the pumps and start mining here." I replied.

"No you're not," was their only reply.

My crew was now suspiciously quiet, and did not offer any argument. I drove back to the where the rest of the gear was and confronted my crew about this turn of events. Their only response was,

"No problem. Don't worry."

"WD, how 'bout coming over there with me. Maybe you can explain better than me how we also intend to help them."

As we approached the site a few hours later, with the truck loaded down with mining gear, we experienced quite a shock. There must have been about thirty Indians lined up at the site, elders (male and female), young braves with bows and arrows and even women suckling their babies. Somehow, this group did not appear to be a welcoming committee.

"Do you feel a little like Custer?" I asked my friend.

"Certainly do," replied WD, with just a hint of uneasiness in his voice.

In the awkward position we now found ourselves, it was essential we portrayed confidence. We got out of the truck and walked up the bank into the crowd, an act that wasn't for the faint of heart.

None of my crew chose to join us, for good reason. The young men and women were yelling at us, demanding that we leave. We stood between the elders and the others, and WD addressed one old man.

"We have come over here to open this pit up for your people. We only ask that you let us work in one small portion of it. With our help you will recover many more diamonds."

One old man smiled and calmly stated,

"No thanks, we don't need your help. You can go now." And that was that. There was no room for argument.

All further attempts to plead our case fell on deaf ears. The elders just stood there smiling and repeating,

"You can go now."

We were now confronted with the dilemma on how to exit the situation gracefully. We turned our backs on the Indians and had a quick strategy meeting and then turned to face the crowd. Then WD said,

"Well, okay. Just thought we could help you get more diamonds."

"Chow," was all the old men said.

We packed our gear and left. I asked my crew why they had led us into such a mess. It turned out that those particular natives were from a more radical community and had previously burnt out a couple of miners. Not all the Pemon communities saw things the same way.

One of the main instigators of this conflict was a young man iron-ically nicknamed 'Canaima'. This was also the name of the Pemon God of Evil and likely, why the lad had been so named. I fired him, which created a completely new set of problems. Shortly afterward, WD's shotgun went missing; Canaima became our prime suspect.

A firearm in the hands of this disgruntled, young man presented a grave danger and had us all a little nervous. Numerous natives in the area had the ability to communicate with those in the spirit world. One of them agreed to assist in finding out the whereabouts of the gun.

After a late night ceremony, which I was not part of, a spirit confirmed that the 'human' Canaima had the gun. The following morning, one of the miners came running up to my camp.

"Jefe, you need to come fast. The 'brujo' got burnt real bad."

A twenty-minute sprint to WD's camp had me facing the sorcerer, who was lying on a bed covered with third degree burns.

"What happened?" I demanded.

"Nothing, go away."

"You need to go to the hospital," I told him.

"No. God Canaima is mad. I cannot go," he replied, his eyes full of fear.

I talked to the man's wife, who was caring for him, and asked her what had happened. Apparently, after discovering who was responsible for the gun disappearing, this man took it upon himself to put a hex on 'Canaima', the native boy. It appeared that the real Canaima took exception to this. As the man conjured up a concoction of gunpowder and other flammables, a gust of wind (on a perfectly calm night) came from nowhere and spread sparks from the fire into the mixture he had between his legs. Now severely burnt, the man was fearful of what other action the God of Evil might take.

I had no vehicle, nor radio, so we had to wait until someone came in from town. Fortunately, the next day a truck arrived, and I was able to persuade the man to accompany me back to civilization to get medical aid. Each day I was becoming more and more aware of the reality of the 'spirit world'. In numerous discussions with elders, I learned that some of them believed Canaima was actually a good God, much like a father. He punished the bad and rewarded the good. If that was true, he had certainly shown his displeasure with the actions of the sorcerer.

Once back in town, I decided to bring Shaine out to the jungle to work for me. His job, for which he would receive one-hundred dollars per month, plus room and board, would entail doing anything I asked. His first job was to start making the churuata (our hut) into a comfortable home. It had no walls, doors, or windows, just a roof to keep off the rain. What it really lacked though, was some shelves to put items on, like pots and food. The first thing that my son had to do was conquer his fears of the foreign insects, snakes and other animals. Once those reservations were mastered, he was able to go forth and gather wood in the jungle. All was going well, until I did something he has yet to forgive me for.

"Shaine, I need to go to town. I want you to stay here and hold the fort."

"When are you coming back?" he naturally asked.

"Tonight, tomorrow at the latest." Being in a rush, I failed to notice the dismay on his face.

I left for town when the next ride came along, and I did not return for three days, as the rains had made the road impassable. Shaine spent three, long, twelve-hour nights alone in the jungle. His only protection from the creatures of the Amazon was a light mosquito net over his hammock. There was no door to close or windows to latch, as there simply were no walls. But the animal that he had feared most, was the lunatic running around with a stolen shotgun. Those lonely nights would surely have unnerved even the most valiant of men. The mind can play horrible games when alone in such dark solitude.

When Shaine described to me what it was like spending those nights lying in the hammock, his mind taking him places he would rather not go, I felt an overwhelming sense of guilt. Worst of all, the sun set at about 6:30 each evening, and didn't rise until twelve hours later, making for a very long night. The chorus of frogs, crickets, birds and the unknown were his only companions in the pitch black of the night. The gathering of the conoto (a magpie like bird) outside the hut in the morning had become a very welcome alarm, signifying the break of day. I never subjected Shaine to another night alone in the wilds, but this initiation to survival in the jungle was one he would surely never forget.

The Pemon Indians do not like snakes, so they set the sabana on fire every year to drive them away. For this reason, there were not many serpents around, but they certainly were not extinct. I never saw one around our campsite, but Shaine killed a non-poisonous snake on the path to the creek during my absence. The mining crew killed a rattler beside their camp one day and placed it alongside the path, with its head propped up in a striking pose. This caused me to do a real double take, much to the delight of the crew. These rattlesnakes were short, fat and very intimidating!

I built an outhouse with a palm roof, using the skills I had learned from the Indians when they constructed my hut. Floyd dropped by one day and had a few comments on it.

"You've got yourself a real snake-pit there Ron. I'd be careful whenever you use it," he said chuckling, but it wasn't long before Floyd was detouring into my place to utilize this unique convenience.

Rick, Tissie and Bubba arrived from Tennessee, and a whole beehive of activity began. Their personal belongings, as well as the heavy equipment, had to be imported and then transported to Sta. Elena. Once everything arrived, they had to place their personal effects into their new home and get the equipment to the head of the trail.

The plan was to fix up the fifty kilometre new trail to the mine in the process of walking the machinery in. This three-week adventure, which required sleeping alone in the jungle with the equipment, would become the most memorable of all my South America experiences.

Chapter 24

STATISTICS PROCLAIM THAT the two most lethal animals on this planet are mosquitoes and human beings. While the former injects deadly viruses, the latter uses whatever means available to inflict harm. The small, white-legged mosquito that spreads malaria, does not fair well in the cooler temperatures of higher altitude. That left man as my primary concern as I traversed the land for the next three weeks.

Although not many miners drove over this new trail, the likelihood of someone stealing our fuel was very real. For this reason I planned to remain with the equipment each night. It would also be an opportunity for me to pursue my spiritual quest. I envisioned nights alone and free of distractions providing me with some quality meditation time. Still, I had no illusions of the potential dangers

Only one trailside robbery had been attempted in this region so far. Would-be thieves, brandishing machetes, jumped in front of a Canadian miner on his way to town. Quickly assessing the situation, the miner stuck his pistol through the open window of his truck and shot several rounds over their heads. They quickly dispersed into the jungle, and in no time word spread that pickings were easier elsewhere.

Some animals have been badly maligned by myth. The poor wolf, despite no documented case of killing a human being in North America, is still feared in the northern forest. (This changed in 2005 when a man was killed in Saskatchewan by a wolf). In this portion of the world, the jaguar was the intimidator. The natives judged me insane for sleeping alone in the jungle, despite the fact that they were unable to recount even one incidence of a jaguar attacking a human being.

To add some credence to their concerns, a huge jaguar leapt in front of our vehicle one day, as WD and I were inching our way along the rutted trail.

"Look at the size of that cat! He must weigh over three-hundred pounds!" exclaimed WD.

"I can't believe how fast he's running!" I said. "He must be doing forty kilometres an hour."

After the magnificent animal leapt in front of the truck, he swerved and ran straight down the road in front of us. Finally, he veered off into the bush and was gone. The largest wild feline in the Americas had just left his imprint on my mind forever.

On another occasion, I had a panther glide across the road in front of my truck. I got very close to this pitch-black animal just before it slithered over some logs and vanished into the jungle.

My claims of seeing a black panther were guffawed in town, so I had to do some research. I learned that what I had seen was actually a black jaguar. The majority of people who lived in the area, including natives, had never seen a jaguar, let alone a black one. I felt truly blessed. Today, in 2007, there are only about fifteen thousand jaguars left in the wild, and the number is declining.

One inhabitant in these parts had a well-deserved bad reputation. The Bushmaster snake made this high, mountain jungle his home and took exception to intruders. They do not like people, avoiding inhabited areas and are fiercely territorial. Normally, both the male and female adopt a small area of jungle as their own. When someone passes through their territory, this aggressive serpent stalks them from behind, and attacks. This is not mere legend. When my friends in the oil industry were cutting seismic line in Bolivia, they had seen the Bushmaster attempt this numerous times. I got a first hand glimpse of why this reptile had such a fierce reputation.

While driving into the mine one day, I encountered a large snake stretched from one side of the road to the other. I came to a stop and the large reptile pulled his gigantic form together into a huge coil. Coiled, head back and ready to strike, this snake was a menacing sight, and definitely not a Boa constrictor! I quickly rolled up my window, as there was no doubt he could strike that high if he so wished. A couple of metres long and over eight centimetres in diameter, I was looking at the largest pit viper in the Western Hemisphere. His arrow-shaped head contained a set of piercing eyes that followed my every movement. The spike on his tail confirmed this was a male, thus accounting for his aggressive nature.

Not a man to leave well enough alone, I decided to inch the truck ahead a little, just to see what he would do. His ferocity was no myth. This huge, highly venomous reptile became airborne, striking my tire not only with his fangs, but also with the stinger on his tail. Although the spike is not poisonous, it still would have inflicted serious injury had it penetrated my soft skin. The venom of the Bushmaster usually causes death in less than an hour, so I truly appreciated the safety of my truck. My philosophy regarding all animals is simple; if they pose no threat and are not a food source, don't kill them. Therefore, I drove away slowly, and watched in the mirror as he slithered into the obscurity of the forest, perhaps sporting an aching fang or two. I now had a newfound respect for the Guaymapiña, the local name for this serpent. Little did I know that we were to meet again, but the next time under quite different circumstances.

Our daily routine normally consisted of young Babba, his grandfather and others coming out to assist me with the road repair. Sometimes Shaine was part of the crew, other days it might be WD, Rick or someone else. In whatever case, it required at least three people to operate the loader, cat and backhoe. We also hired a crew of natives to assist with bridge building and cutting trees down where necessary. With daytime hours filled with noise, people and activity, I looked forward to dusk each evening. At that time, everyone would depart, and I would once more have the wilds to myself.

The real adventure for me started once we got past the village of Betania and away from any form of civilization. Since I established a different campsite at the end of each day, every night fresh sounds resonated from my new surroundings. I never knew that there was such an assortment of frogs, birds and insects, each with their own distinct sound. I slung my hammock between two pieces of equipment, placed my mosquito net over it and hung a black, plastic tarp over my suspended bed to keep the rain off. This was the nature of my home for three weeks. It was rustic, but dry and comfortable.

While this project was underway, my son was relieved of his duties at the hut temporarily. He spread his time between helping us out, aiding Dick, and of course, hanging out in the plaza. The centre of town was where the young people initiated affairs of the heart. Dick managed to get three of the Honda Quad motorbikes licensed to drive on public roads, the only such authorized vehicles in Venezuela. The three gringo boys had an advantage that left the local lads on the sidelines steaming with envy, as they watched their local girls gravitate to the parked quads. This was to cause some unforeseen and dire consequences for the young North Americans.

"Ron, I think you better go to town," Rick informed me one morning when he arrived at my little camp. "Shaine and Michael have been thrown in jail. Dick is busy trying to get them out right now."

I roared into town and found that Dick had managed to secure the release of the youngsters. He proceeded to fill me in on what had happened.

"It seems Ron that the young men in town are a little pissed off. Our lads have captured the attention of all the young girls. One of the boys father is a police officer. It appears that he set up Michael and Shaine, and then arrested them."

"What do you mean?"

"I talked to the Sergeant and he admitted that the officer involved should not have arrested the boys. Anything they were accused of was simply bogus. There was nothing to it. But he did suggest the boys tread a little more lightly."

"Well, thanks for taking care of that Dick. If there's anything I can do, just holler."

That night I had a long talk with Shaine.

"Down here there are some things you have to accept. You're a gringo; you have no rights, nothing's fair and don't expect justice. The best thing you can do is blend in like a blade of grass as much as possible."

"But we did nothing wrong," Shaine argued.

"Like I said........." I threw my hands into the air. Three men and three teenagers – what had we gotten ourselves into?

While in town, I caught up on the local gossip, and discovered that some serious disputes were developing between the North American miners. A common Venezuelan means of battle is using embargoes. This means that one person can accuse another of just about anything, but it is usually takes the form of implied debt. With a properly presented 'gift' to a judge, one person can have another's equipment 'embargoed.' Anything can be placed under this judgement, be it bulldozer or bullshit. The wheels of justice then often grinds to a halt, as does the confiscated property. So now, these northerners were adopting local custom, while I was trying very hard to stay out of the fracas.

These short visits to town were a chance for Liz and I to catch up on everything. Liz often brought home a young child or two for lunch, as many of them were so poor they simply didn't have anything to eat. On one occasion though, she didn't have her normal entourage. This allowed us to have a short but uninterrupted visit. After lunch, I said a pleasant good-bye and headed out the door to journey back into the jungle. About fifteen minutes later, I returned unexpectedly to pick up something I had forgotten.

"Ronaldo, oh thank God your back," blurted Liz, sobbing, as I walked in the door. She was in hysterics, hugging me, crying and talking incoherently. When I finally got her calmed down somewhat, she pointed to the bed.

On the bed lay three sheets of paper, with what appeared to be scribbling all over them. I slowly freed myself from her grasp and made my way over to the bed to see what all the commotion was about. I picked up the papers and started to read what was scrawled all over them.

The first thing I noticed was that it was in English. Not good English, but English. Liz did not speak or write that language, but it was obvious she had written it. It spoke of some mission we were to embark on, to a strange and unknown place, where we would find copper, gold and silver. This was just too weird.

"Ronaldo, after you left, I was getting ready to go back to school. I was heading for the door, when suddenly this crazy, strange, feeling came over me. Like someone was taking over my body, my mind and everything. It was scary. I started writing, although it wasn't me controlling the pen. I don't even know what I wrote. Oh, I'm so glad you came back when you did. I'm scared Ronaldo, really scared."

I spent the next few hours getting her calmed down, and needless to say, she didn't return to her class that day. Upon questioning Liz further, and reading the scrawled message, I came to the only logical answer available. Some spirit, for whatever reason, had invaded her being. What was most strange was that the language of this spirit seemed to have the characteristics of a North American Indian, and that didn't make sense at all. Some of the content of the writings, as well as Liz's description of events, lent serious credence to this assumption. If she had been a person who read or watched movies about the far north, this could have been explainable. But she did not. According to Liz, she had never had any experience like this before, and had never dabbled as a medium or any other such endeavour.

I then remembered something interesting. One of the bizarre things that drew me to Liz was a drawing she had made in her address book, one she had drawn long before she met me. It was of a wolf howling at the moon, titled 'Grito de Salvaje (Call of the Wild). This scene is one that I had treasured for years, and I took this as a sign we were meant to be together. So, why these incursions from the great white north kept making their way into Liz's life, myself included, was strange to say the least. Our natural world was becoming more unnatural by the minute.

I had to return to the machinery before nightfall, but leaving this shaken woman alone in our little cabin was not easy. New to town, she had not yet built a close bond with anyone. Thus, the situation was far from favourable.

With all the complexities in town, it was great to get back to the simplicity of the jungle.

Shaine spent one night with me, and it was on this evening that we encountered a very strange glow-bug. We were sitting by the fire listening to the evening sounds, when we noticed these luminous large insects flying about.

"Shaine, do you see what I see? Old Floyd told me about these bugs, but I didn't believe him."

"Let's see if we can catch one."

Within minutes, I had one of these flying insects in my hand. It was fascinating to watch him follow the contours of my hand, guided by his two mini-headlights. The bug's eyes illuminated his tiny world brightly, and I felt like a giant looking down on a small car. Most amazing was that when he finally flew off, he had a red tail-light that flashed on and off. This was the only time or place I had ever seen such a creature, a truly unique experience.

"I think I owe Floyd an apology," I said laughing. "If we hadn't seen it, I'd never have believed it."

One night of keeping his father company was enough for my son; I was back to camping solo. A few nights later, and a few kilometres further along, I sat once more enjoying the solitude. Sipping some strong, black coffee, I relaxed by the campfire, staring at the starry sky overhead. Suddenly the hair on the back of my neck started to bristle. I wasn't alone. My sixth sense kicked in, as I sensed a presence coming at me from about the nine o'clock position. I stared into the darkness, but my eyes encountered nothing but blackness. To my dismay, I remembered that my gun was in my hammock, too far away to get in a hurry. Picking up the flashlight at my side, I shone it towards the source of the menacing feeling.

There, only ten metres away, sat a majestic jaguar staring directly at me with his huge yellow eyes. So much for the folklore of the cat's fear of fire. When I shone the flashlight in his face, he gave me an annoyed look, then slowly ambled off into the darkness. At first I was dumfounded, but then became quite unnerved. Now what was I to do? Where did he go? Is he circling around to come back and finish me off? My mind was racing and my body trembling.

I grabbed my pistol and crawled up onto the seat of the cab-less front-end loader, shining the flashlight in a wide arc. An hour passed in this uncomfortable position before I finally realized I couldn't stay perched up there all night. I needed sleep. I crawled down off the loader, and placed my black, plastic tarp under and to the sides of my hammock. My theory was that if the Jaguar came for me, he would step on the plastic, scare himself, and at the same time, wake me up. Confident with my innovation, I actually went to sleep, and to my knowledge, the feline did not return.

The many creeks and rivers that we had to cross required some ingenuity. Small log bridges had been constructed to accommodate the width of a Toyota. However, these could not handle the weight or width of our heavy equipment. And so we detoured into the jungle, building ramps of logs in front of us, fording streams and struggling through the thick foliage. On one occasion, the track came off the back-hoe, while going through a swamp. It took us two days and a lot of cursing to remount it.

At long last we found ourselves on the final leg of the journey, skirting the edge of the sabana, yet still in and out of the forest.

"Ronaldo, where are you?" came a welcome sound one morning as I bathed in the creek.

"Down here Liz, I'll be right up."

When I came up from the stream, I found Rick and Liz standing there.

"Great to see you. I didn't expect to see you out here Liz. No school?"

"No, I have a few days off. I thought I'd come out here and see what you were up too. I had to make sure you haven't taken up with one of the native women out here," Liz replied, her laughter a pleasant sound on this beautiful morning.

"Well, give me a few minutes. I'll fold up my tarp and we can get our day under way."

I walked over to the plastic lying on the grass, lifted one end, and jumped back.

"Yeow!" I screamed. "Lookout!"

Staring at me from beneath the tarp was my old friend, the Bushmaster. But, something wasn't quite right. Instead of Rick and Liz reacting in fear, they were bent over in hysterics.

"What the hell!" I exclaimed. "Didn't you see that?"

Slowly, my heart stopped thumping, as it dawned on me why they were laughing.

"On our way in this morning," Rick explained, "we met a crew of miners teasing this snake on the road. It was going nuts, attacking their truck, while we sat back and watched the performance. Eventually they drove over it and killed it. They didn't want it so we picked it up and brought it here. We just couldn't resist having a little fun with it."

"Well, that wasn't funny," I said, still a little shaken. "We've met before, and the last time I saw him, he was very much alive."

This humorous prank was a fitting end to my overland odyssey. I now felt strongly in tune with my surroundings and trusted my instincts far greater. But, the same could not be said for my attempts to converse with God. Was I instead being drawn into the realm of ungodly spirits? My spiritual quest was getting complicated and I was becoming more confused.

Chapter 25

WITH THE HEAVY equipment now on the Codza concession, it was time to bring in Rick's camp. This consisted of a large tent with a wooden platform and all the amenities. He aimed to have comfort, while I chose ambience. Our campsites reflected our different personalities.

It was going to require at least two Toyota truckloads to transport Rick's gear into the site he had chosen. The rainy season was now upon us full force and our feeble road suffered from the torrential downpours. The creeks overflowed our log bridges, making them very difficult to navigate. A daring soul had to feel his way out onto these submersed logs and guide the driver of the truck onto them, with hopefully neither of them falling off into swirling waters.

We overloaded Rick's new Toyota and attempted to go to the mine along the usual route. After nearly falling off one of the log bridges, and several other harrowing incidents, we decided to bring the next load in over an alternate route. Old-timers told us it was lunacy to go that way, especially at this time of year. We soon discovered why.

Right about this time, some friends from Canada paid us a very welcome visit. Wayne, Mary and I had been partners on a gold claim in Northern BC. Since we had already experienced some good times together, it was only fitting that we keep the tradition alive. We were about to experience adventure South American style. Mary wisely bowed out of this one.

With some rough directions on how to access the trail, Rick, Wayne and I set off, the blind leading the blind. We left early, but soon found ourselves lost and meandering across the Gran Sabana. We became further sidetracked by numerous interesting discoveries. One was an outcrop of rock with square cubes, that to this date, no one has been able to identify. Then we happened upon a picture perfect waterfall, with an inviting pool of crystal-clear water. We quickly plunged in and for a brief period, disregarded the fact we were lost.

Reinvigorated, we resumed the search for the infamous self-propelled ferry. Thanks to some wandering natives, we were finally steered in the right direction, and lo and behold, there it was! Beached on the muddy bank of the river sat the rusty contraption, our only means of transportation across the Kukenan River.

Now our only problem was to figure out how it worked. The current would be our means of propulsion, yet the water level was high, further daunting this mission. A cable was suspended across the width of the river, with pulleys and ropes connecting the ferry to it. This would be our lifeline. The one vehicle ferryboat was a metal frame mounted on two long pontoons. Two pieces of channel iron lay parallel the full length of the craft, just wide enough for the wheels of a Toyota to fit in.

"How are we going to get the truck on that thing with the banks as muddy as they are?" Rick asked.

"Carefully," I replied, "Very carefully."

We positioned the metal ramps and then attempted to guide the truck down the bank onto them. It slithered down the slope, and without too much problem, we managed to guide it up onto the ferry. Then things started to get interesting.

"The truck weighs too much. We're stuck on the bank. Drive ahead Rick." I yelled.

As he inched the truck forward, the ferry tipped forward and we slid free of the riverbank. The boat and its cargo began to drift out into the fast moving water.

"We better move the truck back to the middle now," Wayne said.

"Good idea," replied Rick.

We got the truck nicely positioned in the centre of the ferry. This would turn out to be the smartest thing we did, preceding a series of stupid things to follow.

"Okay, now what do we do? We're starting to float out into the river." I urgently noted.

"Tighten up the front rope so we can get the pontoons facing up into the current," Rick yelled.

Since Wayne was at that end of the craft, he loosened the rope. That's when all hell broke loose! The current wanted to take the front end down stream and now Wayne became a link between the rope and the cable. The front of the ferry began to dip down under the water. Wayne's arms were nearly being pulled out of their sockets. Rick and I scrambled forward to help, but with all the weight on the front, the ferry dipped down even more. Water was flowing over the deck, and only providence was keeping the truck from sliding off into the river.

"Give it more slack," Wayne yelled.

When we let the rope slide out more, the front end of the craft bobbed up out of the water and the pontoons at the rear then nosed into the current. In a flash, we were back at shore.

"Now that was a close call!" I exclaimed. I was shaking all over, not only from the adrenalin rush, but also from the physical exertion.

We managed to calm ourselves down, assess our stupidity and then tied the ropes properly. We set off once more, and with the ropes fastened correctly, we whizzed across the water so fast that we literally ran the pontoons up onto the opposite shore.

"Well Wayne, you wanted some excitement. Will that do for now?" I asked.

"Yes, thanks, that'll do just fine. No more of that please."

Our adventures weren't over yet though. Nightfall came and we were still lost. The rain began to come down in torrents and we arrived at a swollen river. Rick wanted to forge ahead, but wiser heads prevailed. We decided to wait for daybreak. We used a tarp to make a tent in the back of the truck and slung our hammocks for the night. By morning the rain had quit, and we now had a chance to assess the river in daylight. We now realized how lucky we were that we'd waited. Just below the crossing was a small waterfall. The high water the night before would have swept us over the falls in a flash. The water level had already dropped drastically from what it had been the previous night. I waded across and tested the depth. It was now fordable, and we made it across without incident. From there it wasn't long before we were back in familiar territory, a little wiser and happy to have survived our ordeal.

The mining began in earnest and we started checking out various prospects. It soon came time to let Shaine go to town for his week off. He surprised me by appearing back at the mine site only a couple of days later.

"Why are you back so soon?"

"I'll tell you later, Dad."

That night, by the light of our campfire, Shaine shared the reason for his quick return.

"I was seeing this girl and thought things were going good. Then her Dad said some weird stuff to me. I ran into Floyd and told him about it. Floyd told me I was nuts to have anything to do with that girl."

"Why did he say that?" I asked.

"I guess her Dad hates Canadians. But more than that, he's crazy. He spends a few months in the nut-house every year or so. Floyd said he wouldn't put it past him to get a Columbian to come and get rid of me," said Shaine. "So, here I am. It's a lot safer out here than in town."

The next day I left Shaine in camp to take care of things. When I returned at the end of the day, he was white as a ghost. Visibly shaken, he slowly related to me the events of his day.

"I was standing here washing dishes, when this helicopter came in real low and right up our trail. I froze. I should have ran, but I just froze. The chopper landed right there," he said, pointing to the spot, "and these guys got out wearing sun glasses. I was sure they were Columbians. They waved for me to come over to the chopper, but I couldn't even talk, and I sure as hell wasn't going over there."

"What were they doing?"

"They just kept motioning for me to come to them; all I could do was look at the jungle and try to figure out if I should make a run for it. Then, I finally understood what they were asking me. They were just looking for a lost lady, saw the hut and thought some Indians lived here."

Sitting back, we had a good laugh about the whole fiasco, but I could imagine the fear my son must have had, given his recent experience in town. His fear was well justified, as solving problems 'Columbian style' was not unheard of in these parts.

With Shaine back, it was my turn to go to town. This time he would not be alone though, as Babba was going to stay with him. My absence over the next few days allowed these two teenagers to get involved in some zany adventures that only the young could come up with.

In town, I got myself updated on local happenings, and joined in the celebration of the President coming to town. Helicopters, military and a festive atmosphere accompanied his annual visit to the area. Liz managed to get in to shake his hand, and I even got a picture of the whole affair. It was pure delight to watch how excited she got over this once in a lifetime opportunity.

It was Easter, so Liz didn't have to work. Her parents came to Sta. Elena for their first visit, and we had a great time touring around to different scenic spots. We took them out to our little retreat in the jungle. Her father, seventy-three years old, quickly took to looking for diamonds with a saruka, a backbreaking process that even I couldn't maintain for any length of time. Liz's Mom, at fifty-three years of age, adapted quickly to cooking over an open fire and sleeping in a hammock. They were such pleasant and unassuming people to be around. Their natural curiosity pulled into focus things I hadn't noticed before, especially certain plants, birds and insects.

The refreshing interlude soon ended, and I transported Liz's family back to town. While they rode a bus home, I bounced my way back out to Codza. On my return, Shaine updated me on his latest shenanigans.

"Dad, you won't believe what I went through when you were gone," he said.

"Now what," I replied, assuming I was about to be assailed with a new set of problems.

"After you left with Liz and her family, Babba and I took the Toyota over to WD's camp. It started to rain hard, so we headed back to the hut. That crazy Bubba slid off the logs on that creek over there."

"How did you get out of there?"

"It was totally dark and I walked the two miles over here in the pouring rain to get the front-end loader. The worst part was crossing our creek in the dark. The water was real high," Shaine said, his voice expressing the fear he had known.

"You walked across that in the dark when it was high like that?" I asked incredulously.

"Yup, got the loader and went back and got Bubba out. Did you know there are no lights on the loader either? So I drove back in the dark."

I could hardly believe what he was telling me. When it rained at night, it didn't get any blacker. Yet with only a weak flashlight, he had managed to make this three-way journey safely. I had to believe there was more than just a little luck with him that night.

"That's not all. Bubba, you tell him," Shaine said.

"The other night I snuck up on WD's crew to see if they were stealing the gold like you thought. Well, they were. But I made some noise and they caught me. They let me go, but threatened me not to tell anyone," said Bubba.

I had assumed right. We had a serious problem. WD had one of the best crews in the valley, and the majority had been with him since the beginning. He was in town, so the responsibility became mine to handle the situation. There was only one recourse.

"Maturin, you and the crew pack up your stuff. You guys are finished. The cook too. After all WD's done for you and you rip him off? You're outta here!" I snarled at WD's captain.

I soon became very nervous about having a bunch of disgruntled miners hanging around the valley, so I borrowed a Toyota, loaded them up and took them all to town. We stopped at the alcabala and the guardia started a thorough search of their belongings. This had never been done to this degree before, and I took exception to the process when they went to check my bags.

I stepped forward, pulled a pen out of my pocket and started writing down the name of the guardia officer reaching for my bag.

"What are you doing?" asked the sergeant from behind his desk.

Ignoring the armed guards surrounding me, I walked over and slammed my hand down hard on the sergeant's desk.

"You have no right to go into my bag, and the embassy will be given the name of anyone who goes into it. If anything is missing, that fellow there will be responsible," I yelled.

The commotion caused the guardia to bring their machine-guns to the ready position, and the Lieutenant came storming out of a back room.

"What's going on here?" he demanded.

As luck would have it, I knew the Lieutenant. When I explained the situation to him, he told me to carry on; that was the end of that. My outburst gave the locals one more reason to perceive me as a 'loco' gringo, but this had to be one of the craziest things I ever did. The fact that I wasn't shot on the spot had to be Divine intervention. God must have been shaking his head at my stupidity as He bailed me out of that one.

Although WD was now without a crew, he agreed with my handling of the affair and soon put together another crew. I returned to the jungle and let Shaine go to town. Once again, he was to face more dramatics.

I received a message that I had better go to town, so I caught the next ride in. Shaine quickly updated me on the latest events.

A couple of jealous, local, young lads strung a black cable across a road that they knew Michael and Shaine would zoom down with their quads after dark. As fortune would have it, that particular night they were driving slower than normal, and when they ran into the cable, they were not decapitated. Shaine received a cut on his face, and Michael had managed to get the quad stopped with the cable pressed tight against his throat. Matters were starting to take on very serious proportions.

A police investigation found the two fifteen-year-olds who were responsible, but since they were youths, not much more could be done. This did, however, expose the gravity of the situation to the young, teenage gringos. What they would need to do was form some friendships with the young men of the village, instead of being their adversaries.

On top of all this commotion, I received notice that the Commandant of the Guardia Nacional wanted to speak to me.

"Señor Johnson, your son has been involved in an illegal activity. He took some fuel with one of those Honda's up into the hills. This was used to help Señor Chris escape with the helicopter that was under embargo," the Commandant told me.

"I was unaware of any of this, but I'll check into it," I replied, and this seemed to satisfy the high-ranking officer.

I confronted Shaine and asked what this was all about.

"Dick asked Michael and me to take the fuel up to the top of one of the mountains with the quads. We didn't know why and he didn't tell us. He just said to do it. I didn't see any chopper when we were there."

It didn't take much investigation to find out who was responsible for the phoney embargo, and for the Guardia Nacional's involvement with my son. I confronted the guilty Canadian at a local dance. Liz got scared and left my side, as she had never seen that look in my eyes. Nose to nose, I informed the person responsible, that if it ever happened again, there would be dire consequences, not only him, but for all those involved. My eyes must have conveyed the sincerity of my words, for he and his bunch caused us no further grief.

One night I asked Liz if she would be interested in delving into some mysticism to try to find out what we were supposed to be doing. This would involve inviting a spirit into our home and Liz acting as a medium. She was not very receptive to this idea, as she had no experience with this other than the uninvited one that invaded her being some time before. But with some coercion, I was able to convince her it would be worth the effort.

We made a little shrine in our cabin, lit some candles and went into heavy meditation. It did not take long for a spirit to take advantage of this opportunity. Liz's face and demeanour changed dramatically, and Juan introduced himself.

The exact words he said now escape me, but in a deep and strange voice coming forth from Liz's lips, he proceeded to inform us about certain financial concerns we should have. Unfortunately, this transformation of Liz's physical body and voice scared me so much that I lost sense of why we had done this in the first place. I broke the trance by boldly informing 'Juan' that we no longer needed him. My interruption worked and he left, leaving Liz shaken, crying and not at all impressed. This had not been one of my better ideas.

I returned to the jungle and tried once more to enter the realm of the supernatural – I'm a slow learner. The night was calm as I sat by my campfire and proceeded to call upon my spirit guide to make his presence known. I pursued this relentlessly for some time. Suddenly a whirlwind burst into my little setting and swept through the fire, spreading sparks over the roof of my hut and all around. The atmosphere was heavy and foreboding. I screamed,

"Stop, stop! No more. That's enough!"

As quickly as the torment began, it ended. I jumped up and extinguished the threatening sparks on my roof. Shaking from head to foot, I finally realized that I had overstepped my boundaries. My dabbling in mysticism had to end now.

I reverted to proper prayer. From the depths of my soul, I asked God for some divine guidance. This time, the message was very clear and lacked the dramatics I had previously encountered. It was time to leave the Gran Sabana, and Venezuela. I was getting involved in things I knew nothing of, and the incidents involving my son were getting worse day by the day. If we didn't leave soon, someone was going to get seriously hurt.

Shaine returned a couple days later and I informed him of my decision.

"No way Dad, I'm not leaving. You can go, but I'm staying," was his surprising response. Here was a kid who had to wash his clothes with a scrub brush in the stream, cook over an open fire and pack water up from the creek to wash dishes. On top of this, he had no TV, radio or music of any kind, and yet he vehemently insisted on staying in this primitive setting.

"Please go up on the hill there and have a talk with God," I said.

Reluctantly, he left the camp and walked off into the darkness. An hour or so later he returned.

"Okay Dad, guess you're right. When are we going?"

"Well, I have to let Rick and WD know. I have a standing job offer to go to work in Algeria. I can make some good money there and get back on my feet. The worst part is how Liz is going to take this. I want to take her to Canada, but I'm not sure if she wants to go."

"Well, whatever," said Shaine, and the decision to leave Venezuela was made.

Chapter 26

"P OR QUE?" Liz screamed at me.

"Liz, I'm broke. We just haven't managed to hit the right spot for the diamonds. I'm tired of watching you eat rice and not knowing where the next meal is coming from."

"What about me?" Liz asked. "Can I come to Canada with you?"

"That's what I hoped you would say. Of course you can, although not right away. It will take time to get immigration papers ready. I think we should get married, and that will make it a lot easier. Do you want to marry me Liz?" I asked.

"Yes, yes, Amour, I do," she readily responded.

One down, two to go. Next person on the list to inform of my major decision was my best friend and partner, WD.

"Ron, I fully understand. You have to take care of yourself. Don't worry about me," WD said when I sheepishly told him of my latest resolution.

"Well, I can't tell you how hard this is for me. I love it here, and you have been one super friend, but there comes a time… Now, to break the news to Rick," I lamented.

Rick, understandably, was a little less forgiving. He was upset with my decision, as he had been relying on me to run his operation. But a man's gotta do what a man's gotta do, and I had just done it. I was grateful for WD's support through this time, as my head was in turmoil knowing how many lives I was affecting by my sudden decision. He assisted me in finalizing things, and most important, gave me the moral encouragement I needed.

We put together a quick wedding, and with Shaine present, Liz and I got married in a civil ceremony on June 28, 1996 in Sta. Elena de Uairén, Venezuela. One week later, Shaine and I were on a plane to Miami, leaving behind my anxious, new bride. My promise to Liz was that once I was financially stable, and her immigration papers were in order, I would bring her to Canada. For the time being, she would have to exist on the pittance she received as a teacher's aid and the little cash I was able to leave with her.

I arrived stateside in tattered jeans, with neither a watch nor even a jacket. The culture shock to both Shaine and I was immense, and it took a couple of days in Miami to assimilate. I managed to squeeze a bit of money out of my maxed out Visa and made myself presentable. Then it was on to Canada.

Right away things started going askew. My new job entailed going to Algeria to assemble camp shacks for Western Geophysical in the middle of the Sahara Desert, but there was one slight problem. The ship carrying the building material to Algeria seemed to have disappeared and no one seemed to know its whereabouts. Now, all I could do was wait until the wayward ship was discovered, and the goods were delivered. Fortunately, my new boss was able to provide me with a place to live, as well as employment in a hardware store in Northern Alberta.

Although the wages were minimal, it allowed me to survive while we waited for rectification of the shipping problem. During this time, I began the process of applying for Liz's immigration papers. Now I was in for a real shock. Had I brought her in as my secretary on a visitor's visa, there would have been no problem. However, as my wife, she would not be allowed into Canada under any circumstances until formal and complete immigration was finalized. I made calls to Ottawa and the Embassy in Caracas, but to no avail. When she set foot on Canadian soil for the first time, the government demanded that she arrive as a full immigrant. This caused extreme aggravation for both Liz and I.

Liz made a two-day trip to Caracas and went through all the immigration processes there. This was extremely difficult for her, as it meant staying several days in the city with friends and trying to find her way around. Once there, the proverbial run-around began. Little consideration was given to her circumstances, and she was at her wits end. Despite this, she completed the required documents, which the government subsequently lost. She was then told that she would have to go through the whole process again. That was just too much for Liz and she informed me she was no longer interested in coming to live in Canada.

Meanwhile, I was back attending my twelve-step meetings and trying to get my life back in order. My spiritual quest had taken a frightening turn in Venezuela, so I now sought a more realistic path to God. My residence on a lake gave me a lot of time to work on this.

"Dad, why don't you come and work with us," Shaine said to me one day. He had begun to work for a friend of mine at a natural gas plant.

"Yes, it looks like this dream of working in Africa has fizzled. I'll give Ron a call."

Ron quickly offered me a career as an operator at a gas plant. This new job meant working in the bush for one week, followed by a week attending school in town. Slowly my brain cells were reactivated as I learned physics and other subjects long forgotten. My new job was exciting and invigorating, and I felt that I had once more found my niche. Then winter arrived. Riding around on a snow machine in the northern cold checking gas-wells was a stark contrast from the heat of South America. So, when my first employer called, and said the goods had reached the Sahara, I was once more on the move. These resolutions weren't ingratiating myself with people, and although Ron was understanding, he was also disappointed.

On December 23, 1996, I found myself in London, England, wandering around in a daze suffering from jet lag. I took video pictures of Buckingham Palace and many other sites, just to ensure myself that I really had been there. I hadn't slept for two days.

We left Beacon Hill airport on an executive jet and flew directly into the centre of Algeria. Terrorism was so bad in Algiers that it was not a safe place for any westerner. Once in the country, we boarded a small Pilatus airplane and flew east into the Sahara for two and a half hours. I would not see a female face for the next two months, nor would I see a tree or any form of civilization other than camel riding nomads. Sand dunes surrounded me, stretching for as far as the eye could see.

The mobile camp we were constructing required my learning carpentry, wiring and plumbing. I was surprised at how cold it was in the mornings, at times near freezing. By 11 am, the heat was getting intense. We quit work at 5:30 every evening, and that was when I would hike up into the dunes and attempt to reconnect with God through some serious desert meditation. This daily ritual slowly brought me back into a very positive relationship with my Higher Power.

It was during these meditative reposes that I began to get a strong sense that my pursuit of all things Venezuelan was ill conceived. These feelings grew stronger each day, yet I could not figure out why. A whole host of miracles were about to make it unmistakably clear what I was supposed to do. Time passed quickly and soon it was time to return to Canada and then on to Venezuela.

"God, I have been like a tornado in people's lives. If I am to make another drastic change that is going to affect others, please make it for the good and simple for me to see." This was the basis of my prayers while flying back to Venezuela.

My arrival at the little airport on the old DC-3 did not fill me with the normal elation of coming home. Rather, I felt a deep foreboding that I could not pin point, nor shake.

"Ronaldo, I'm pregnant," was the shocking news Liz had waiting for me. "I didn't think you were coming back. All my friends said you wouldn't. Even your friends. Then, one night, when I was lonely, a nice fellow I met convinced me that you wouldn't be back." Liz's crying overtook the moment.

I was flabbergasted. Before we even started a relationship, I had made it clear that I couldn't father a child due to a vasectomy. Liz informed me that the doctor said she couldn't have children, and these facts played a major role in our decision to pursue the relationship. The time element and my operation made it quite clear who the father wasn't.

Then I remembered my prayer on the plane. This certainly seemed like an awful way to disentangle me from my responsibilities. Emotions ran as rampant as the tears that followed. This was not easy on her or me. However, the course of action I now had to take seemed exceedingly clear.

My days of living in Venezuela were ending, and now all that remained was finishing the final chapter. Although Liz wanted me to accept the baby and its ramifications, I felt that this was the door I was given to exit. I took Liz home to her parents, and with many heartfelt tears and final good-byes, I left for Margarita Island to lick my wounds.

I spent three weeks alone on the beach praying and trying to decipher what was God's will. Feeling hurt and betrayed, I attempted to sort out my emotions. My love for Liz, coupled with a sense of responsibility, made the message extremely confusing. In the end, I knew I had to follow that inner voice and accept that I was not responsible for the way things had turned out. So, back to Caracas I went.

When I had arrived in the country, I had given my passport to Western Geophysical so that they could apply for my next work visa to Algeria. I went to their office to get my passport. It was lost! No one knew where it was. The woman who had sent it out was beside herself with despair. I tried phoning my boss in Canada, but he was on the road travelling and unavailable. Now I had another dilemma. Besides the emotional turmoil I was dealing with, I found myself trapped in Venezuela with my funds depleted. I had left Liz with most of my cash, and now my credit card was over its limit. With no passport, I couldn't even board my unredeemable flight back to Canada.

Down to my last sixty dollars, and one night left in a cheap hotel room, it was time for some serious prayer. My passport had been missing now for three weeks.

"God, you know my situation better than even I do myself. Please help me get out of this country," I prayed, with intenseness like never before.

I made my way once more to the large company's office, my feet instinctively finding their way there, while my mind immersed itself in worry. I entered the office and was shocked when the secretary jumped up from behind her desk, ran around and gave me a big hug, with tears rolling down her cheeks.

"It' here, it's here," she exclaimed in Spanish. "I don't know where it came from, but this morning it came."

"Gracias, gracias," I said, not only to the relieved woman, but also the One responsible for this miracle.

I took my passport and new work visa for Algeria and went to the plaza. I sat there letting the reality of what had just happened set in. Once I realized that God was really listening and answering my prayers at the present moment, I decided it might be wise to make further use of the Divine connection.

"God, I thank You from the bottom of my heart for answering my last prayer. I don't want to sound selfish, but if it is in Your heart to get me out of here, can I please have some direction how to get home to Canada?"

I silently prayed on a park bench while hundreds of people strolled by. A message in my head kept telling me to go to the travel agent and use my Visa to get a ticket home. I, of course, argued back that my credit card wouldn't work since it had been over limit for some time. But the voice persisted, so I simply followed the instructions.

"I would like to buy a one way ticket to Peace River, Alberta," I told the smiling travel agent.

I handed her my Visa and held my breath. I figured why go half-way, book a flight all the way home, not just to North America.

In just a few minutes, the lovely woman handed me my Visa, and my ticket.

"Have a nice flight." I was so glad there is no quota on miracles.

As I sat on the plane flying away from my home of the last five years, the power of prayer was all I could think of. With a heart full of gratitude, I was glad to be once more connected with the God of my understanding.

Epilogue

The recent miracles in my life opened a completely new awareness, and I began to take note of all the little 'coincidences' happening, not just once in awhile, but all the time. I returned to Algeria for another two months and then decided it was time to pursue my spiritual journey. I went to retreats in Encinitas and Hidden Valley, California, with the Self Realization Fellowship. When I disembarked the plane in Calgary, I felt like a new person. I had become a non-smoker and tasted a sense of freedom I had never known.

It is hard to explain why one doesn't continue doing what feels good, but I slowly slipped away from my blissful life and reverted to old habits. I drove truck for a year throughout North America and then one day received an exciting phone call.

"Ron, how would you like to come to Peru? We have a super opportunity happening here, and sure would like it if you were to come on down," was WD's encouraging request.

"What are you doing there?" I asked.

"We are starting a gold mine operation and plan to build a processing plant."

It didn't take much encouragement before I was off to live in Nazca, Peru. Somehow, I forgot the clear message I had received back in Venezuela and flew Liz back into my life with her young son, Miguel. Maybe I just needed to extinguish some guilty feelings for my part in disrupting her life.

Cultural differences and other factors made for a tumultuous time that culminated in us finally parting ways. This time I no longer felt guilt or responsibility, as I had done as much as possible to provide a good life for her and Miguel. A lot of pain could have been avoided had I not forgotten the message so clearly given to me back in Venezuela.

Timing is everything, and although WD and I accomplished most of our goals, politics eventually caused our demise. The price of gold sitting at two-hundred and sixty dollars per ounce, coupled with the instability of the Fujumori election and his subsequent ouster, were all factors out of our control

I loved Peru and the people, but could not maintain my financial stability by sitting on hold waiting for the situation to change. Back to Canada I returned once more, this time to stay.

Today, residing in Chilliwack, BC, I have a lovely woman in my life, Shirley, who has her feet firmly planted on the ground. She is patient, understanding and most of all, has shown me what unconditional love is. Her adventurous spirit compliments mine, and together we enjoy meeting new challenges.

Happily re-immersed in my twelve-step program of living, life has become a whole lot simpler. My spiritual quest has brought me full circle back to the God of my own understanding, who has patiently been at my side all along. Balancing my persistent desire for adventure with the rewards of serenity is an ongoing process. The more my drumbeat comes in tune with God's, the smoother the journey.

MZ

ISBN 142517917-7

9 781425 179175